O9-ABI-663

HOW TO WIN AT POKER

How to win
at POKER

BY JOHN MOSS

Garden City Books

Garden City, New York

Garden City Books edition by special
arrangement with Knight Publishers

Copyright, 1950, by Knight Publishers
All Rights Reserved
Printed in the United States

A NOTE ABOUT THE AUTHOR

It would be well to begin this biographical note by saying that there is no such person as "John Moss." This name hides, for obvious reasons, the identity of an astute midwestern poker player.

"John Moss" was born and raised and has spent the forty-three years of his life in Detroit, excepting four years in the armed forces of our country. He took his degree from the University of Michigan at Ann Arbor, preparatory to spending his adult life as an investment counselor. An abiding interest in certain features of mathematics as well as in the law of probabilities led him to experiment with the frequency of cards falling in particular ways, and he found to his surprise that his early training in various card games had helped him develop a natural ability as a card player. His father, it might be noted, was a first-rate bridge and whist player, first in New York and later in Detroit.

Mr. Moss's interest in cards quickly concentrated on poker and became increasingly absorbing until he found he was spending more time playing poker than in pursuing his academic work. Simultaneously with the receiving of his B.A., Mr. Moss was forced by the severe depression of 1932 to earn a living for himself and his family by any means at his command. Men trained in banking and investment procedure were a dime a dozen in those days—as many of us recall only too well. At any rate, part-time poker had afforded a modest but steady income during undergraduate days, and the straitened circumstances of his family together with his natural affinity and liking for poker led him to abandon his business plans and devote himself exclusively to this fascinating game.

His rise to pre-eminence was almost immediate. Today, John Moss is recognized (under his true name) as one of the country's really fine poker players.

This book offers no infallible guide to winning at poker, nor can it make a winner out of a hopeless dub. But it will substantially improve the game of virtually every reader, providing him with insights he previously lacked.

Here is an authoritative statement of first principles, of the basic facts of poker. Beyond this point no book of instruction can go. The rest is up to the abilities of individual players. Certain psychological factors enter into the play—factors which it is beyond the scope of any book to analyze, because of variations in every case. Poker is an individual game. To lay down standards for the psychological aspects of the game is to ignore the accepted fact of definite variation in individual behavior and conduct. Such cut-and-dried principles might work one night but grievously backfire the next.

We have carefully examined other poker books available today. As average players ourselves, we were concerned with improving our game. None of the available books quite filled the bill. Some of them were written chiefly or entirely for use by table stakes and pot limit players and contained little of solid interest to the limit player. Others were too often inferior or inadequate, and, occasionally, downright misleading. The need for an authoritative book was clear. Drawing on our army friendship with John Moss we persuaded him to prepare this study.

Poker is played regularly by countless millions of people. We hope they will all find this book to be what, in fact, it is: a thorough, intelligent, exhaustive guide and textbook on how to play and *win* at poker.

THE PUBLISHERS

FOREWORD

I am a self-considered piscatorial perfessor with limitations.

Cyprinus carpio of the family of *Cyprinidae* is commonly called Carp. I am not original when I say that it is the most heartily despised fish that swims the American waters.

Mr. Ray Bergman, a famous authority, has written, "Without a doubt the Carp is one of the most wary fish that swims and it requires the utmost skill to effect the capture of a mature specimen." That may accurately describe old *Cyprinus carpio* but it is a far cry from the only Carp that interests me.

I am very fond of the two-legged variety. He is often called a "poor fish" or "sucker" but I prefer the more loving term "Carp," for it suggests, according to Mr. Bergman, wariness and great skill. The surest way I know to clip a poker player is to assure him he is very skillful at the greatest of all card gambling games, for that induces carelessness and over-betting.

I know a brilliant sales manager who is a pushover at poker. He jabbers away almost constantly about business or his family but when he gets a good hand the salesman comes out. "Who dealt?" he asks. "Did you stay? How much can I bet?" etc., etc. When he starts that lingo, I quit. I know he is loaded for moose.

Another pal of mine could never arouse the interest of his dog or even hail a taxicab with his whistle (for he had none). But he always puckers his lips and puts forth weird hisses which he apparently intends to be music—whenever he thinks he is about to make a killing.

An old telegraph operator I once knew would set down at the table for a game of chance. He would fill his mouth full of Beechnut Chewing Tobacco but movement of his jaws came only when he had a good hand. The harder he chopped the more careful one had to be to survive. At poker that old-timer was real vicious.

The characters mentioned above are not really the Carp type, because their only weakness is psychological. But the individual who gurgles, "I just love to play poker," and "Have you ever played Spades Wild?" is the kind of mental cripple that must be likened to the finny tribe. If the game lasts long enough he is bound to lose.

There is no reason to suspect that *How to Win at Poker* by John Moss will cause the disastrous disappearance of the two-legged Carp, for in his own stupidity the Carp imagines he knows everything about poker and he wouldn't consider attempting to improve his game. But for anyone who really desires to play the game well for money, marbles or matches, I suggest a reading of this masterpiece.

It is not only the best book ever published about a pastime dear to millions; it's the only one ever written that I consider worthy of your attention or mine.

W. W. GOODPASTURE

CONTENTS

Odds against improving your hand in draw poker (see back cover)

INTRODUCTION

Generally speaking, there are two kinds of poker games—social poker and poker for blood. Everybody knows what social poker is. A bunch of people sitting around the dining-room table playing for pennies, with deuces, fives and tens, one-eyed jacks, and anything else wild that the dealer thinks will liven things up. The games are spit-in-the-ocean, baseball, rollover (Mexican stud), low-hole-card wild, up-and-down the river, and innumerable other variations on the same theme. This is social poker. Everybody has a good time, and nobody gets hurt. Full houses are a dime a dozen, and five of a kind is held every fourth hand.

The other game is blood poker—or, if you prefer, poker for keeps. This is a money game, played chiefly by men, and somebody gets hurt nearly always. Somebody else goes home a winner. It is the purpose of this book to send you home ahead of the game.

Two kinds of money poker

Blood poker further divides into two kinds. One is the real big money game—table stakes and pot limit—played by rich people and professional gamblers. The other—and more common—is *limit poker,* and it is played by millions of men and women. The limit can be dime-quarter, quarter-half, a dollar, two and four, or whatever figure you want to set. It is usually "dealer's choice," which means the dealer can call any game he wishes—draw, stud, etc. The principles of correct play, as outlined in this book, are applicable equally to nickel-dime and $50-$100 games. Players find their own financial level and play on it. A game in which you can bet up to $50 per card, with $100 on an open pair or on the last card is just as much a limit game as dime-quarter poker. You need more money to play in the bigger game, but because everyone in the game can afford the stakes, money is nullified as a factor, and principles of strategy and tactics will determine who wins and who loses.

This is not a book for the table stakes or pot limit players. There are already books written especially for them. They play quite another game of poker than those who sit in the limit games. Bluffing becomes a most important factor in the biggest games. In limit poker it is still important, but not so vital, because it is hard to run a successful bluff for a quarter. More of this later.

Second, as to the types of games that are dealt with: well, there are only two basic poker games—five-card stud and draw. (In this book, the term "draw" refers to a form of draw known as Jack Pots—i.e., it takes a pair of jacks or better to open the betting. In my experience, most of the draw poker played in limit games is of this type. One rarely finds draw played in a limit game when one can open "on his nerve." Hence, all draw situations and discussions in this book are meant to apply to Jack Pots—or "jacks or better" to open the betting.)

The wide acceptance of seven-card stud as a fine limit poker game has led me to include it with the first two.

The man who loves poker is satisfied with these. They offer him all of the variety he wants. Those who sometimes play variations—such as six-card stud—will find most of the principles and much of the strategy still applicable. These variations aren't dealt with in this book, partly through lack of space, but mainly because they aren't the real gambling games. If you don't find enough challenge and stimulation in these three basic poker games, either you don't play well enough, or poker just isn't your meat.

There are other games that are popular, among them lowball and high-low, but these again are bastard games, with little standing among the men who know poker and play as experts. Poker offers unlimited possibilities in the three types discussed herein. Why bother with any others (except socially)? How often have you seen professional gamblers playing high-low? You might as well ask them to play deuces wild.

Concentrate on the standard games

My advice to those of you who have been playing a dozen different poker variations is to concentrate on these three games. Master them. Try to get the others in your group to stop clowning around with high-low (a game in which the pot is divided between the highest and lowest hands) and similar varieties.

One thing I can't give you is card sense. A lot of people claim there is no such thing as card sense, and I don't propose to argue the matter here. But there is definitely a certain intuitiveness in the make-up of an expert card player. He senses what the others are holding. He senses the way his own hand will unfold, impossible though it may seem. This is a highly developed sensitivity to cards. And whether you call it card sense or by some other name, it is still an important factor in poker. It seems most common in those who have grown up with cards, playing all sorts of games since they were youngsters. If you lack it you aren't severely handicapped, but it will help your play if you possess a certain amount of it.

Another thing I can't teach you is alertness. You've got to stay on your toes. Watch the other players. Watch their cards. Remember the cards that showed in a hand that has folded. When you fold early in a hand, get up and walk around. Catch some fresh air, if possible. Don't get sluggish. In the long run it will help you win. Train yourself to look once at your hole cards and to remember what they are without having to look again.

Develop a style

Develop a style of play and stick to it. But don't be too consistent. If you invariably squeeze out your last card in a seven-card stud, the others will know that when you don't squeeze it you're already in and don't need it. Vary your play. Sometimes you should stand pat with two pairs—or draw only one card to three of a kind. Hold a kicker occasionally. Other times—most of the time, in fact—you should not make these draws, but play the hand right, taking the full number of cards to your holding. But it doesn't pay to do it always that way, otherwise everyone will know what you went in with.

For example, a man who never holds a kicker will always draw three cards to a pair. Thus, if he draws only two cards on a hand, everyone knows he has three of a kind. Now look at it the other way. If he usually drew three to a pair, but sometimes held a kicker—then, when he had his three of a kind and drew two cards, the others wouldn't know whether he held a pair and a kicker or three of a kind. And this is important when it comes to getting callers. You want the other players in there calling you when you have a strong hand, and you can't expect them to stay when they know they're beaten. This is the advantage of varying your play.

Let's take another example. If you always refuse to bluff your unsuccessful one-card draws—so that the others know you will not stay in unless you've hit—you can't expect them to call you when you draw one card and bet or raise; *unless* they've got full houses. That's why it is important to bluff a hand now and then. They won't know whether you're bluffing or not, and likely they'll stick around to see. But if you never try to run a bluff, they'll get out in a hurry when you stay.

It is the threat of the bluff that is so deadly. A very large percentage of all the calls that are made shouldn't be made—were it not for the chance that the bettor is bluffing. When opener checks to a one-card draw, and one-card bets, opener may call with jacks, not because he thinks he can beat one-card, but because he wants to make sure one-card has what he says he has.

So it's the threat that one-card might be bluffing that keeps the opener in there and impels him to call. If one-card has never been known to run a bluff, opener will fold without calling, feeling pretty sure that one-card caught. Most poker players have an unholy fear of being bluffed out of a pot that is rightfully theirs. It's a mistake for them to think this, of course, because they'll lose a whole lot more calling hands they can't beat than they will win by catching bluffers. But that's the way most players are, and you should take advantage of this fact by keeping them guessing.

Bluffing in limit poker

If you do carry through a successful bluff, don't let it go to your head. Remember this: there is very little money won by bluffing in limit poker. How often can you expect to win a pot on nothing when it takes only a quarter or a half dollar to call? In table stakes, it's another matter altogether. Here there are many bluffs, and they are often successful. But that is another game. In limit poker there are very few successful bluffs. The thing you want to remember about bluffing is that you want to get caught! Then, when you hold a strong hand, the others will recall that you have been known to try a bluff, and they will be in there calling.

You bluff in limit poker to instill a fear of bluffing in the others. You can't figure on making much by trying to steal pots, unless you're playing with men who have just learned. If in the course of an evening you try five bluffs and two of them work, you will be very little ahead. You've lost the three times you were called. Furthermore, you are never going to bluff a big pot. The only reason the pot got big is that the others had enough to call or raise. You can't drive them out after the last card. Not all of them. Somebody is certain to keep you honest. So, as far as those five hands are concerned, you are probably even. But those five bluffs will pay off many times in the fat pots you will win on those hands when you are loaded and everyone calls because they're afraid you are bluffing.

A single bluff

Perhaps the simplest bluff in all poker occurs in five-card stud. It is carried out by a player who wants to win the ante. The best limit for this bluff is a dollar. If the high man bets a quarter, you, sitting on his immediate left, make it $1.25—no matter what you show. The others will not know if you have a pair wired or an ace in the hole. You can count on dropping everybody, except those with pairs at least as high as your up-card and maybe those with a high up-card and an ace in the hole. This raise will usually fold most or all of your competition.

But bear in mind that you don't stand to win much by this bluff—

the ante and the first man's bet—and that if you have callers you may easily lose. Still, this is a popular form of bluffing that satisfies those with a penchant for bluffing. The less the difference between the amount of the first bet and the amount of your raise, the harder it is to win the bluff.

These points—and many others—are discussed more fully in the pages to follow.

Poker may not be the social game for both sexes that bridge is, and it may not be the 100% intellectual pastime that chess is, but it is a truly democratic game that tops all others in psychology. You are an individual, playing without a partner, strictly for yourself, and responsible to no one for your mistakes. In addition, poker can be a profitable diversion for you. With proper play you can figure on coming out a winner over a period of time, and just about everybody can use those extra bucks.

So here's wishing you good luck—and stay away from those inside straights!

JOHN MOSS

HOW TO WIN AT POKER

CHAPTER 1

Poker etiquette—thirteen rules of conduct

1. Before you deal, always offer the cards to the man on your right to cut. This is an important part of the etiquette of poker. Also it is clear indication of your honesty. Even if you are playing in an informal game in which the cards are dealt without being cut, offer them for the cut when you deal. It is well to get in the habit of doing things right, and it will help you to play more naturally in another game in which the rules are closely followed.

2. Deal the cards down, holding the deck close to the table, with the front of the deck turned down slightly. This reduces the chances of your flashing a card. In addition, players watching for their own cards in draw or their down cards in stud do not like to see what they are going to get. They want to squeeze them out, and this is their privilege.

3. Shuffle the cards with care, making particularly sure that, after a hand in which three of a kind showed, the cards are well mixed. It is always annoying to the others to have the three kings of a previous hand come one after the other in a hand of stud.

4. Call the cards as you deal them. When dealing the first round, call: "queen," "seven," "jack," etc., as you deal the up-cards. On the second round, announce the hands: "queen–six," "jack–nine—two spades," "pair of sevens," etc. Always call every pair and call all possible straights or flushes (three cards showing is enough to make the holding possible). After dealing the round of up-cards, designate the first bettor with the statement: "pair of sevens bet" or "ace bets," etc. This speeds up the game. While every player normally watches the fall of the cards, the dealer should call each holding as he deals.

Don't peek

5. Never, never peek at cards coming up in later rounds, even though you are out of the hand. This is a bad breach of poker etiquette and causes distrust and ill-will. Nor should you permit anybody else to peep at cards still in the deck that will be dealt in the next round. The suspense of a critical hand may be intense, but that does not excuse riffling through the deck to see if that flush is going to come in.

6. Even though you are out of the hand, do not attempt to look at any other player's hole cards or watch him squeeze out his draw, unless he states that it is all right for you to do so. If he has anything, you'll see it soon enough anyway, and by waiting you will not antagonize anyone. Needless to say, after having been given the courtesy of seeing another man's holding, you must not give any indication of the nature of his hand. Nor should you then look at anybody else's hand.

7. Under no circumstances should you attempt to see the hand of a player who has bet and won the pot when no one called. This is inexcusable. The whole idea of poker is to get others to pay to see your cards, and whether you are in the pot or not you have no right to look at an uncalled hand. If, for example, a man opens and has several callers, draws three cards and bets and no one calls, he must show his openers, but you are not entitled to see his other cards. Remember, though, that when a hand is checked* or called, all players in the game (whether in this particular hand all the way or not) are equally entitled to see every hand—both the winning hand and the others. Thus, if somebody asks to see your cards after the hand is over, you are bound to show them, regardless of whether or not you won the pot, provided the hand was either checked on the last round, or there was a bet and you were a caller.

*"Check" and other expressions used in different localities all mean the same thing: I'm staying but not betting (no one else has bet).

If you drop out before the last round, you are not required to show your cards to anybody, and doing so is a courtesy only. You may, of course, refuse. But it is important to remember that everybody has an equal right to see every hand on a checked last round or to see all of the caller's hands on a bet-and-called last round. If there is a bettor and no one calls, no one in the game is entitled to see the winning hand, and to try to see it either openly or as you pick up and arrange the cards is in very bad taste and upsets the game.

Stay alert

8. Do not delay the game. Bet promptly when it is your turn. If you raise, say it so that the others hear. If you fold, turn your cards at once. No one is entitled to ask what up-cards you folded, and you should not answer, as it is unfair to the other players. Some will have noted your up-cards before you folded, and if a player who failed to do this can ask you what you had and get an answer, there is no longer any premium on alertness. But bet, raise, fold, and check in turn. Do the thing right! Doing any of these out of turn disrupts the game. It is unfair to the other players. If you fold out of turn it has a psychological effect on the other players who are still making up their minds what to do.

Betting out of turn is careless and unfair to the others. If you raise out of turn you are likely to hurt yourself, because it often means those who might have stayed for the original bet and then felt forced to see the raise will fold up, glad to have saved some money. All of these admonitions may seem elementary, but the fact is they are violated repeatedly by hundreds of thousands of poker players. Learn to play right! For all its seemingly informal nature, poker is an exacting game, with an etiquette comparable to that of golf. Do it right—and insist that the others do so. No game can survive sloppy play. No one enjoys a careless game as much as he does a correct one. Discipline yourself to play properly; it will help your game.

Remember each draw

9. Do not ask how many cards anybody drew in draw poker. The dealer should announce each draw—including his own, if he stays— and it is up to the other players to be alert and notice what each man takes. Very often one finds instances such as this: opener draws three cards; B draws one; C two. Opener bets, B raises. C folds. Opener turns to B and says: "How many cards did you take?" B, of course, is not required to answer this question and should, in fact, remain silent. It is the opener's hard luck, and he is not entitled to an answer. Nevertheless, B often answers out of courtesy. In my opinion, this is unfair to the other players (when there are others in the hand), and, in any case, the opener is taking advantage of B's sense of fair play. It is quite true that in most cases, if the situation were reversed, the opener would answer the question as to his draw. But it is not good poker, and it makes for a sloppy game. If you refuse to answer when asked, others may do likewise, and soon you will have strengthened the game generally by making the players conform to this rule. One way to stop such questions is to give a wrong answer. Tell the man that you took two, when you took only one. It may not be exactly ethical, but neither is his question—and it will eventually discourage such questions.

10. Don't beef about your bad luck. Nothing is more annoying in a poker game than to have some guy grousing about his bad luck all the time. No one cares to hear about your bad luck—or that you haven't won a hand for an hour. No one is sympathetic—any more than you are when somebody else is grumbling. Learn to take the bad luck with the good, and don't throw the cards around, or complain unduly, or make a nuisance of yourself. It's never easy to sit and lose money, but everyone has to from time to time, and if you learn to lose gracefully it will not only make you more welcome in a poker game, but will put you in a better frame of mind.

11. Never criticize the play of others, either to them personally or to a third player. If a man makes a poor play, note it for your own future reference, but don't embarrass him by calling his attention to it. A man should be entitled to lose his own money any way he wants to. You should rejoice in bad plays you see around you. But don't talk about them.

Don't be unreasonable

Nor should you complain to the man on your right that he should have stayed (when he folded and your card dropped on the immediate left) or folded (when he catches the card you want). This is silly, of course, but many players do it constantly. Even when he stays on nothing in a hand when he should have folded, and catches your card, you should keep quiet. Good players don't complain about such things, but many not-so-good ones do. It is always a man's privilege to stay or fold as he wishes, and you cannot expect him to do anything except in the interests of his own cards and himself. His rights are equal to yours, and no matter how correct your raise was, for example, and how little he was justified in staying in, the fact is that if the raise fails to fold him and he then catches a card you wanted, you should still keep quiet about it.

12. Ante in turn, and get the others to do so. The pot will be found to be light sometimes, and everybody will insist he is in. Perhaps each player thinks he really is in. But somebody is light. Anteing in turn will prevent such needless situations and misunderstandings.

13. In draw poker, when you take one card to a straight or flush and fail to catch, don't throw in your hand until the betting has reached you. (I shall dwell on this repeatedly in this book, because it is most important and yet is violated repeatedly by far too many players.) It is unfair to the others for you to fold out of turn. Whereas the opener might check to your one-card draw, if he sees that you didn't catch he may go ahead and bet. Then the other players who hoped to have the round checked will have to pay to see the bettor. They resent your folding out of turn, because it makes the hand more expensive for them. If the betting is checked to you, you must check, too, even though you failed to catch. You cannot fold until somebody has bet and it is your turn to act. The same applies to stud poker.

Similarly, with any holding you must fold in turn. Suppose somebody bets and a second man raises (whether draw or stud makes no difference). If a man folds out of turn it is bad psychologically for the others. Beyond any question, anybody who cannot learn to play by the rules should not sit in any poker game. Though it is an individual game, all have equal rights.

CHAPTER 2

General advice, tips, and comments

The necessity of preserving a poker face has, in my opinion, been greatly overemphasized until now it is stressed far beyond its true importance. Naturally you will not be well-advised to grin broadly when you catch, or frown and sigh when you miss. Nor can you expect others to do so. But, whereas facial muscles can be controlled and, thus, deliberately used to deceive, certain nervous habits are unconscious, and precisely because they are involuntary, you will learn a lot more watching another player's actions, for example, than you will his face. I suggest that if your face sometimes betrays your hand, you refrain from looking at your draw or at that seventh card until it is your turn to bet.

On any particular hand, the man's conduct may be an exception to his usual behavior, but you will usually be able to rely on your observations and profit accordingly. Watch to see if the man who regularly sweats out his last card squeezes it out or looks at it casually. The former will generally mean he needs to catch; the latter that he was already in.

Watch, particularly in five-card stud, how often a man looks at his hole card. A six, for example, is harder to remember than a king. Having once seen an ace or king in the hole it is unlikely that he will look again. But be careful of the conclusions you draw in this connection. Don't assume too much. Simply note the fact and bear it in mind. As other facts assemble this may be decisive. Remember, too, that as the evening progresses most poker players become less alert and are likely to take a second or third look at a hole card they would have remembered with only one look two hours earlier.

If you have never known a man to bluff—and there are those who, through an excess of timidity or caution, never do bluff—you may take his raise to indicate a strong hand. Thus, you may fold or only call where you might otherwise call or raise. But there is always a first time, and if this is one of his very rare bluffs, you are losing out on a hand you might have won. If it is a bluff and is exposed, you must immediately revise your mental notes of this man's play.

Who is likely to bluff

For whatever it may be worth to you, it is my experience that the man who is losing, particularly if he can't afford to lose much, is much less likely to bluff than the man who is about even or a little ahead. Similarly, the man who is well ahead is not likely to bluff, unless he is a bluffer by nature and is attempting to make his extraordinary luck seem to be holding out. This type of player, when ahead, is likely to bluff a one-card draw, figuring the others will think he has caught again and will win. Don't get too worried about others bluffing. Bear in mind that it is very difficult to carry through a bluff in less than a quarter–half game—actually, a dollar limit is about the lowest limit that allows constant bluffing chances—and most of the potential bluffers in your game will have been burned enough times trying to run bluffs in small limit games that they aren't interested in trying any more. If the game is full of fish (i.e., weak players), however, the potential bluffer may come to life.

Speaking of fish, while they have certain advantages, such as staying around and contributing when they should have folded, they also bring an element of uncertainty to the game. They are forever making extraordinary draws, and their play suffers from a confusing inconsistency. Not a deliberate inconsistency designed to keep the other players guessing, but an inconsistency caused by their uncertainty and lack of experience and knowledge of the game. You cannot expect to drive them out with strategic raises, for example, as you might reasonably expect to do with good, sound players. They will stay in there and outdraw you. Or try to. If they do, don't beef. Console yourself with the thought that they will wind up losing because they are going to be in there trying to outdraw you dozens of times—unsuccessfully. Their two favorite tricks are to stay in a stud hand with nothing and catch a pair on the last card to beat your ace high, or catch a high pair to beat your fives. And they are forever staying in draw to take three cards and catch to a pair of fours or any small pair that better players would have dropped like hot potatoes.

Beware of poor players

Fish have certain disadvantages for you that stem from their lack of experience. For example, when they are high, after a round of betting in which some player raised, they are likely to bet into the raise, either forgetting that the man raised or being unconscious of that raise. This is disadvantageous to the other players who would like to stay, but sitting between the fish, who bet, and the man who raised the last round, they must either fold or call and chance the raise. (Naturally this does not apply to those instances when the fish—or anybody else—improves on the card he just caught and bets into the raiser, deliberately, hoping for a bump.) In a sense, there is a conspiracy against every raiser. Those who stay in are anxious to get by as cheaply as possible—until they hit—and they will all check, as if on signal, to the raiser. Thus muzzled he can only bet and they then call. But, a fish can mess things up for you by betting automatically when he is high. Bear this in mind and play accordingly.

One word more on fish. As a rule they are tough to bluff in limit poker. They can be counted on to call. Just as they are hard to drive out, so they are the most difficult players to pull a fast one on. They figure they came to play and to see five (or seven) cards, and that's what they do. You can't drive them out with a cannon. You cannot expect them to fold in the face of nothing. They are the prototype of the Missourian who said "Show me!" They feel—many of them—that it is the world's worst disgrace to be bluffed out of a poker pot that is rightfully theirs, and they call and call and call. The most perfectly conceived and executed bluff imaginable folds the expert, but the fish is in there to the bitter end. Remember: your bluff is based on several factors such as the ability of the others to read cards, their fear of a powerful hand, the way you have bet the hand thus far, other cards that show, etc. The fish can't read cards at all, is positively fearless—raising kings full with his fives up with an easy confidence—has no idea how you have bet the hand thus far, and never looks at the exposed cards of other hands to draw conclusions from them. My own advice is to stay out of games in which there are fish. They never know when they're supposed to bet, slow up the game, and louse things up generally. Unless they have plenty to lose it's not worth your while to play poker with them. But, if you insist on doing so, or find yourself in a situation where this is unavoidable, treat them with caution usually reserved for experts.

Be liberal—to a degree

Don't play too tight a game. In the average limit game, every man is entitled to play as he feels is best, but a certain liberality is expected. This doesn't mean that you must make bad stays or calls. It means that poker is a game which offers more than money, and if all you care about is money, you won't be welcome in many poker games. Not that everybody isn't trying to win, because of course they are. But relax and enjoy yourself occasionally. Stay when this book says fold. For myself, the four-flush is the most irresistible holding in poker. Even though the odds may not be favorable, I usually draw to it—except in the big games—and I expect to continue doing so. It is a form of indulgence I permit myself.

My only warning is, don't form any bad habits. Don't, for example, get in the habit of staying with a small pair in draw. It will be too expensive. But, if in the course of an evening you want to draw to a pair of eights, do so. I know this sounds exactly the opposite of the title of this book, but, in the long run, it is beneficial. It tends to loosen you up a little, relax you, take some of the tension off so that you'll be in better shape for the big hands when they come. Just don't get careless. My suggestion is that you do as I do and draw to the flushes, even if only a couple of others have stayed. Of all the one-card draws, this offers the best chance of hitting, and you can figure to win if it does come in. On the other hand, if you get in the habit of drawing to a small pair, it will be expensive for two reasons: first, you won't improve enough times to make it worth while, and as you will often hold one small pair on the deal in draw, drawing to them is an expensive proposition; and, second, even if you do improve, you may not win the pot, because somebody else may improve, too. This gets even more expensive. On the other hand, the four-flush doesn't come round too often to be an expensive holding, and when you draw to it and hit you will usually win. If you don't hit you don't have to worry about calling.

Don't be a change-maker! This is particularly true if you play with money rather than chips. If a man plays light on a ten dollar bill, don't offer to change it. If he wants change, he'll ask for it. Many players are superstitious and don't want a bill changed. They prefer to play light on it, thinking they may win the pot and recover it without having had to break it. When a man pulls out a bill, he is often losing and going into the sock. The last thing he wants is an offer of change, for he resents having to break the bill and resents you, particularly, because you are a winner and therefore able to break it for him. In addition, making change seems to show a certain greediness on the part of the man who makes it, and this doesn't sit well with the others. When you are ahead, don't make change unless you are specifically asked to do so. Don't break a bill tossed into the pot. Leave it there. Everybody likes to win a pot with a five-spot in it, and the players in the hand all want that fin. They don't want anybody pulling it out and dropping five ones.

Poker manners

Remember that you must be more careful of your conduct when winning than when losing. A loser has a certain license to beef about his luck, and others, while never sympathetic, will take it without getting sore. But when the winner beefs about his luck on any given hand, they resent it. Under no circumstances brag about your winnings. This is rubbing salt on the wounds and is bound to build ill-will. I have run into only a handful of poker players in my years of play throughout the world who would not have been outclassed— and I don't mean financially—in a game somewhere else. Poker playing ability is like strength. No matter how strong you are there is always somebody that's even stronger. So don't be a bad winner.

Put a copy of Hoyle in your coat pocket before you go to join the boys for a game. It will be most helpful if arguments arise. What happens, for example, if a man opens, several stay, and play progresses to the point where, after the draw, the opener folds. Asked to show his openers he finds that he didn't have those two pairs after all. What now? This, and similar points, can lead to long arguments and hard feelings that disrupt the game. Buy a copy of Hoyle or poker rule book (see *Oswald Jacoby on Poker* [Doubleday]) so that you'll know the score.

Watch the one-card draw

The following points are of interest:

1. In draw, when you have opened with kings, let us say, and catch a third king to make three of a kind, you would normally bet the hand (unless you feel you can sandbag). If there is a one-card draw, however, it is always advisable to check. But before checking, watch the man who draws one card. His actions may indicate whether or not he caught. Often the one-card drawer will throw down his hand when he failed to catch. If he does this, it is not dishonest for you to take advantage of your knowledge that he didn't catch and to bet your hand. It has been argued that many players are in the habit of putting the card they draw to an inside straight in the middle of the four they hold and putting the card they draw to a bobtail straight* on the outside. In my experience, just as many don't do this as do, and I don't think it can be argued either way.

Bear in mind, also, that many one-card draws are to two pairs—even though the player may not have raised in the opening round. A raiser who draws one card is usually holding two pairs or three of a kind, and less often a four-flush. Only rarely does a player raise on a bobtail straight . . . and if anyone in your game raises on an inside catch for a straight, you ought to have his shirt by closing time.

2. When, in draw, a player calls and draws two cards he is usually holding a kicker. If you, as opener, hold two pairs, jacks up, and check them and the two-card draw bets, you can only call and are almost surely beaten. Only an ace or king should be held for a kicker, and his bet indicates aces or kings up—or better. You can only call with your two pairs. If another man has opened and checks to a two-

*Open at both ends.

card draw on your right, and the two-card draw bets, don't call with less than aces up or three of a kind, because his bet will almost always mean aces or kings up, and perhaps more. With a high three of a kind your proper bet is to raise, unless there are several possible callers still to be heard from.

When the opener checks

3. When, in draw, the opener checks, it ordinarily will mean he has either improved only slightly or not at all. If there has been a one-card draw, however, he is probably checking to it as well. If there is no one-card draw, and the opener checks to you, bet with any two pairs—or with aces and a king kicker—unless there are at least two players on your left still to be heard from. In the latter case, you must check too, as your two pairs may be beaten. But, if the opener and several players on your right check, then bet. The chances are that it will cost you nothing, because if a player on your left calls, he would probably have bet if you hadn't, and you would have certainly been forced to call, partly because you think you may have him beat, and partly because no one else is likely to call. If you bet, however, it is most unlikely that he will raise. (But do not bet into a one-card draw.) If he does raise you may safely figure him for three of a kind—or more—and if anyone else calls, fold with anything less than aces up.

4. The subject of bluffing is always a touchy matter to discuss in a book of this sort, and no matter what is said on this delicate subject it cannot be considered 100% accurate or inclusive, because bluffing will vary with the game limit and the players.

As has been mentioned earlier, it is very difficult to run a successful bluff in limit poker. A bet of ten cents or a quarter or a dollar isn't likely to drive anybody out who can't see that he's beaten in sight. To try to run many bluffs in limit poker is, therefore, dangerous, and it rarely pays off. A bluff can be set up and executed perfectly at the exact psychological moment, yet fail simply because the expense of keeping the bettor honest is so slight. So I say to those who want to steal an every fifth pot: don't try. It is costly and fruitless.

More on bluffing

However, as the limit increases—up to the dollar maximum we are discussing in this book—bluffing becomes more practical. Certain types of bluff, often successful in dollar limit poker, have been mentioned and explained elsewhere in this book. But there are a few principles which can be established in connection with your own bluffs and those of the other players: first, the big loser is the least likely bluffer, because he doesn't want to take any undue chances. There are exceptions, of course, but my experience tends to bear this out. On the other hand, the big winner is usually a potential bluffer. He has made so many bets and raises all evening and been called—to win with a full house or three of a kind or some other strong holding— that the other players feel he probably has another winner and fold.

This man is often likely to push a possible flush—possible, that is, in view of his up-cards in seven-card stud—even though he has nothing in the hole. If he shows two spades, raises on that round of betting, and catches another spade on the next round, he will have the respect of the others. They will check to him. If he determines to bluff the hand—i.e., has no spades in the hole—he may find it advisable to try to sandbag this round, if he is high. Or to raise someone else's bet, provided his raise comes at a time when most of the other players haven't contributed on that round of betting and may therefore be driven out by his raise. Beware of the raise that comes from such a holding after the others are in. It will usually mean at least one spade in the hole, and far from being a bluff, such a bet would be one designed to build the pot. The raiser is betting on the come.

Certain players are more easily bluffed than others. Never for a minute get the two types mixed. If you do want to bluff, make your effort against a man who is likely to throw in his hand, rather than the man who always calls as a matter of habit.

Harder to bluff a weak player

Provided your bluff is properly handled, it is always easier to bluff a good player than a bad one. The poorer player is usually a bad card reader and, therefore, unimpressed with your holding. Furthermore, he often calls automatically, tossing in his money as a matter of course. This is because he feels no one should be allowed to steal a pot, and he wants to keep you honest. You can't drive him out. Set up your projected bluff so that this "old reliable" is likely to be knocked out by a raise in the betting during the preliminary rounds. If you go down to the wire with him, you may as well forget the bluff, because he is sure to be in there calling.

Another reason a poorer player is harder to bluff is that he often feels it is humiliating to be bluffed out of a pot and will gladly pay money to avoid such embarrassment. The reader of this book, who will become a good player if he isn't already, should not feel concerned about being bluffed out. Don't let yourself be bullied out of the hand, but if, in your opinion, the cards seem to indicate a stronger holding is out, don't permit any personal sense of obligation to force you to call. Get out of the hand. If the man has bluffed you, so what? You played it as you saw it. Next time he tries to bluff one you may be sitting with kings full. But don't feel bad about being bluffed out. It's happened many times to all of the world's great poker players. It will happen many times more. A man who can be bluffed—not constantly, but now and then—is going to win more than the man who always calls. Because the man who always calls simply to keep from being bluffed is not going to win one hand in thirty that he does this on, for the reason that relatively few bluffs are tried in limit poker.

At the same time, it is always advisable to vary your game. Try to run a bluff yourself now and then. If it is unsuccessful and exposed it will help assure callers the next hand when you may have a legitimate winner. Similarly, keep the other players honest from time to time. If you don't you'll find they come to know that you won't keep them honest, and they'll steal a number of pots. Play the cards at all times. Refuse to be intimidated, no matter how powerful the opposing hands appear. Often their bark is worse than their bite. Alertness and card reading are the surest ways to keep from being bluffed.

Ask yourself these questions: What did he show when he first raised? What has he caught since then that might fit with what he showed at first? Has he been raising on later rounds? Have what seemed to be good cards for him fallen to other hands? How many spades (or whatever suit he may show several cards in) can you account for? Does my hand show its real power? Do the other hands show power? (Raises into hands showing pairs and possible straights and flushes are usually legitimate—in limit poker—because the bettor knows it is unlikely he will drive out those who already have something or have excellent possibilities.) Is he winning? or losing? Is he a bluffer as a rule? (Regarding this last, you will find that some players in the game invariably have strength when they raise, no matter how weak and unpromising their exposed cards may appear. Others frequently bet on the come and on hunches, preferring to push their luck. Often the bluffer will have what looks to be excellent possibilities and his bets and raises seem natural enough. Sometimes he won't decide to try a bluff until after his straight or flush has failed to come in.)

Bluff 'em out early!

One last word on bluffing in limit poker: the successful bluff will almost always be carried out before the hand is over. That is to say, the bluffer will succeed in driving everybody out before the last round of betting. If he fails to do this he will usually fail in his attempt to run the bluff, because he can figure that whoever survives the betting and raising earlier in the hand will not collapse in the face of one last bet. Thus, the successful bluffer must raise when the first bettor is on his right, making it doubly expensive for those still to come in. In the face of such a raise they are inclined to fold if they have nothing.

Rule: Generally speaking, try only enough bluffs yourself so that you can be assured of callers when you have a strong hand and want them. Limit poker is not a bluffing game. For every pot you can steal there will be a dozen that you will lose.

CHAPTER 3

Draw poker—do's and don'ts

Draw poker offers only two rounds of betting—however many raises it may contain—and this means that you must make both rounds count, playing for a raise whenever possible.

To begin with, let us state a few principles that are generally applicable:

1. Don't open first or even second hand with minimum openers. Some players prefer to check always with jacks or queens, others only when they are under the gun. It will depend partly on the number of players in the game—the larger the game the better advised you will be to check minimum openers under the gun. As a general rule this is sound strategy. If you open first hand with jacks, someone may raise, and you could have avoided paying double simply by checking. If the hand should be checked out, don't worry about it. There's always another hand, and you must be satisfied to know that you played the hand safe. If someone else has openers and opens the play, you can stick around safely, able to draw to your minimum holding with a minimum bet.

2. Don't raise immediately on the left of the opener, unless you hope to drive the other players out and win the ante.

Some players are willing to raise on a pair of aces when they sit on the opener's right and there have been no raises. Their theory is that the opener is the only man who may be going in with a better hand than aces—because had anyone else held more he would have bumped. Feeling that they have as good a hand as anyone, they raise.

While I can't recommend this practice, I am not inclined to criticize it too severely. But there are specific dangers. One is that the opener may have a strong hand and bump immediately. (Or he may just call, to assure keeping the others in.) Second, a man on the opener's left may be holding a strong hand and bump back. His failure to bump originally is explained by his unwillingness to risk driving the others out. Third, there may be some dangerous one-card draws (to flushes and bobtail straights) out against you—and if they hit you are probably beaten. It is a gambling bet for aggressive confident players. It is not infrequently suicidal.

Fold with less than jacks

3. Don't stay with less than jacks after the pot has been opened. This is the *minimum,* and one would not be ill-advised to fold even jacks. With queens or better, stay. To draw to a small pair is simply to invite losses. You will catch a second pair only about once in every five draws—and even when you do catch you can lose the hand. I can only repeat my earlier statement: if you insist on throwing in money to play with poor cards, you must expect to lose. A good poker player throws away smaller pairs repeatedly, and will draw to them only when he is playing a game in which the ante has been repeated a number of times, as no one was able to open, and he can protect his previous antes with a small bet.

There is no excuse for a man staying with a small pair to play when the pot has been opened and raised. Nevertheless, one sees this done many times in the course of the evening—invariably by poor players. If you weaken and stay with a small pair and some later bettor raises, you should fold. The old rule about throwing good money after bad is definitely applicable here. Nor can you blame anyone but yourself for having been put in such a position, because your correct play was to fold originally.

4. Don't hold a kicker—except occasionally to vary your draw or because of some unusual circumstances which will only rarely occur. It is a good policy to draw occasionally two cards to a pair, holding a kicker, or one card to three of a kind, to give the impression you were drawing to two pairs. If, sometimes, you hold a kicker, and the other players know you are in the habit of doing this from time to time, there is no need to draw only one card to three of a kind. The reason for this is that, when you draw two cards, the other players will not know whether you are drawing to a pair with a kicker, or drawing to three of a kind. The player who absolutely refuses to hold a kicker should vary his draw to three of a kind, sometimes taking two cards and sometimes one. Otherwise, the other players will be able to place his holding every time.

Check to one-card draws

5. Don't, as a rule, bet into one-card draws. There are exceptions to this, of course, but it usually holds true. The man may be drawing to a flush or bobtail straight, and if he catches, you are sure to be bumped. At the same time, if you hold three aces and have four stayers, including one who draws one card, a bet may be in order. Bear in mind the type of player the one-card drawer is. Does he often draw to inside straights? If so, perhaps this one is, too. With the possibility of getting four calls to your aces, it may be worth while to risk the raise you will catch from the one-card if he has hit. At the same time, if you check, perhaps the others will, too, and you are not capitalizing your aces. Let's say you check, the one-card draw folds (or checks) when his turn comes—if he didn't catch, whether he folds or checks will depend on whether there is an intervening bet—and a man bets. You should raise, unless you can hold the others in better by calling. Knowing that the man drew at least two cards, you must not be worried about having your three aces stand up, and you can safely raise. I realize, of course, that sometimes he will be full and you will be beaten. Nevertheless the raise is sound.

6. Don't fold, when your turn to bet comes, and everyone has thus far checked. Even though you drew to a small pair and didn't catch, so that you know you are beaten, or drew without success to a four-flush or a four-straight, your proper play is to check. This is only fair to all of the others in the game, and it may be important should some-one wish to run a bluff. Fold only when you do not want to call a bet already made. Fold in turn.

Do not throw in your hand after seeing that your one-card draw failed, until it is your turn to bet. This is most important, and is only fair to the others in the game, because the opener may be watching you closely, and when he sees you throw in your hand he may bet— knowing he does not have to fear the one-card draw—when otherwise he would have checked. This premature folding hurts the others, who may have high pairs and are hoping to have the round checked so that they can have a shot at winning without paying. The players in the game should insist on everyone folding and betting in turn.

7. If you wish to sandbag (i.e., check a strong hand, then raise when someone else bets) before the draw, you should be right under the gun. Check your strong hand, hoping that another will bet. When he opens, raise. Remember, however, that the man who does open (if anyone does!) may be the player on your right, in which case your re-raise may drive the others out. I do not as a rule recommend sandbagging before the draw. Calling—then raising when somebody else has raised is another matter. Nor should a man raise on a four-flush unless at least five other players have already stayed. The odds are roughly 4½ to 1 (9 chances in 47) that you will not catch, and to raise if there are fewer than five is giving yourself the short end of the odds. As a matter of fact, I do not advise staying to draw to a four-flush unless at least three have stayed. This is advice likely to be ignored—for a four-flush is almost irresistible—but this is a book on how to win at poker, not how to have a good time, and I cannot honestly advise drawing to a four-flush when the money odds aren't equal to the mathematical odds of catching.

The bobtail straight

Never raise on a bobtail straight. Never draw to a bobtail straight, unless there are at least four others in the hand. Again you will be giving yourself the short end of the odds if you persist in drawing to bobtail straights with only two or three other callers. (Your chances of catching are 8 in 47—or about 5 to 1.) It is pleasant to catch to these one-card draws, but they are costly in the long run unless the money odds are good.

Never draw to an inside straight. Well, almost never. Your chances of hitting are, roughly, 1 in 12, and it is foolish to attempt it. I can conceive of a situation in which one might be justified in making the one-card draw, but it is unlikely to arise more than once in a blue moon: If holding A-K-K-J-10, the man on your right opens and you stay, and he stands pat on the draw, you might be justified in making the one-card draw to the inside straight, provided you had played with this man long enough to know that he almost never bluffs—this is a favorite bluffing play—and that he never stood pat with less than a pat hand (i.e., never with two pairs). Here you may as well draw to the inside, knowing full well as you do so that even if you catch you may still lose (to a flush or full house). Had you known he was pat you could have dropped at once. But now that you're in the soup, heroic measures are necessary, and you may as well make the draw. Your chances of making it are slim indeed, but your chances of improving the kings with or without the kicker, to the point where they have a chance against a pat hand are a great deal slimmer. But I can suggest only this or a similar circumstance as justifying drawing to an inside straight. I mention it only in passing as a thought to those who insist drawing to an inside straight is never justified. In this example, incidentally, if the slightest doubt exists as to whether the pat hand is really pat, by all means draw to the kings and take your chance.

CHAPTER 4

How to play two pairs in draw

The most perplexing holding in draw poker is two pairs.

Playing other holdings is almost always a cut-and-dried matter compared with the problems faced by the man with two pairs. When holding two pairs, if the man on your right opens, by all means bump. You will have to do your raising before the draw, because, holding two pairs, it is important to drive everyone out as quickly as possible. The reason for this is that your chances of improving with the draw are very slim. There is only one possible holding you can improve to—a full house—and the chances of your filling up on a draw to two pairs are about the same as your chances of catching to an inside straight, roughly 11 to 1. For this reason, you should bet heavily before the draw, and, if you fail to improve, check after the draw.

Much will depend on where you are sitting. If a man on your right opens, an immediate raise may force those who have not already bet out of the hand. Thus, the number of those who will be drawing to a pair and, perhaps, outdrawing you, is reduced. If you open the betting and catch a raise from a man on your left, call when it comes around to you, unless you are holding a strong two pair (e.g., aces up). If you open and a man on your right raises when it gets around to him, raise back with two pairs. This will make it pretty expensive for the others, and while they are in for something already, some will fold rather than throw in twice as much to protect their original call.

If you opened and everyone stays, but no one raises, check, after the draw, unless you fill up or have aces up. This is simply protection for your hand. If you open and draw one card, the other players know you hold either two pairs or three of a kind, and if any of them catches three of a kind, he may bump you and will certainly win. You have little to gain by betting, and will often lose.

And when you fill . . .

If you fill up and there were three or four callers on the opening round, sandbagging may be in order, and this is a matter you will have to judge for yourself. As an opener drawing one card, you will be placed with either two pairs or three of a kind, and anyone with a fairly high three of a kind is likely to bet into you if you check, giving you a chance to bump back. As a matter of fact, if, as the opener, you draw one card and check, the others will figure you for two pairs almost invariably. Thus, if you do fill you are in a position to exploit their underestimating your hand. Don't be afraid of having no callers when you check. If there is a one-card draw made by someone, your checking a full house may seem to be deferring to the one-card draw, and it will lead the others to believe that your best possible holding is three of a kind, and more likely, two pairs. As a result, if the one-card draw checks, too, any player following it who has caught three of a kind is apt to bet, and you will be able to raise.

If the one-card draw bets, you have a good bump, but you must only call if he re-raises, unless you have a very high full house. The reason for this is that he may have drawn to two pairs, too, and filled. When you open and draw one card and then raise another one-card draw, you are stating very clearly that you hold a full house. Thus, the man who made the one-card draw is not likely to kick back unless he, too, is full, and with a high full. With aces full you can raise once again, but if he also raises, you must call, figuring he drew to a straight flush and caught or drew to four of a kind. If he held three of a kind in the beginning and held a kicker, catching four of a kind, you will be beaten, of course, but, in view of his failure to raise in the first round, you cannot figure it likely he holds four of a kind.

If another player has opened, and you bump with your two pairs, drawing one card, your hand will be partially hidden. For there is a possibility you are holding a four-flush or a bobtail straight and bumped on the come. When you bump and the others call, the opener is likely to check to you after the draw—whereupon you, too, must check, unless you have filled up.

Check—or bet?

The purpose of your raise before the draw was not to sweeten the pot, but to drive the others out. It is unlikely that you will drive out anyone by betting after the draw (anyone, that is, who wouldn't have gone out anyway), and there is no point in your betting—and losing —when a check may save money. However, you must expect that when you check, those coming after you will figure that you failed to catch, and they will become bolder in their betting. If anyone of them caught three of a kind, he will surely bet. If he caught a high two pair he will probably bet. Consequently, you may prefer to bet yourself—holding a high two pair—because you can feel quite sure that no one will raise the bet of a one-card draw. This is strictly a matter of preference. Checking is always safer. A bet by you will not drive out any three of a kind hand. It may drop a player holding a small two pair—but nothing more.

However, it is not unlikely that your two pairs will win the hand, particularly if it is a high two pair. Kings up, for example, will usually be a winner in draw poker. Consequently, you must call any bet, unless there is a bet and a raise. This will almost certainly mean that someone is holding three of a kind or more and you can safely fold. For every time you stay in and win, there will be a dozen when you are beaten, and in the long run it is an expensive proposition calling such bets and raises.

Somebody may raise

If the man on your right, the opener, bets after the draw, and you call, and a man on your left raises, drop if the opener calls or bumps, but call if the opener folds. This is very important when you have, say, aces up. The man who raises may have drawn two or three cards.

Perhaps he holds queens up. When you simply call the opener's bet, he figures you for two pairs, and thinks his two pairs are higher. Admittedly, it is unsound play for the opener to bet into the one-card draw—particularly if he is so weak as to be unable to call the raise of a hand that drew two or more cards—but such things happen (sometimes the opener will forget you drew one card), and you must know your proper play. More often you will be beaten, if anyone can raise the openers, and I do not recommend calling with less than kings up. With, say, tens up, you should fold, whether the opener calls or not.

If the opener, on your right, checks to you and you check with kings up, and the man on your left bets, you should call, regardless of what the opener does (unless the opener was sandbagging and raises). The opener may figure you will fold when it is your turn and may be keeping the bettor honest with nothing more than openers. Similarly the bettor may figure you drew to a straight or flush and failed to catch, so he will bet the two pairs he holds.*

Under the circumstances your proper play is to call—unless the opener or someone else bumps. If the opener was sandbagging, you fold. If someone else raises, you fold, because it is doubtful that two pairs can win the hand. Either the bettor or the raiser is probably holding three of a kind or better. Perhaps both are. But, in any case, the raiser has probably figured the bettor for at least two pairs, and it is doubtful that he would bump with less than three of a kind.

Don't draw to small pairs

It is a mistake to stay in draw poker with less than a pair of jacks or tens—with the exception noted below—and if you persist in doing

*Here again I should emphasize that the only one way to play poker is by the rules. Therefore, let me repeat that no one should fold his hand under any circumstances until two things are true: (1) it is his turn to act; (2) there has been a bet made, and he must call, raise, or drop out. If the betting has been checked to him, he must not fold if he didn't catch. He must check, too. Only when a bet has been made is he allowed to fold—if he doesn't wish to call—and then only in turn. Too many players, drawing to small pairs or to a straight or flush throw in their hands as soon as they see they didn't improve or catch. They feel, logically enough, that inasmuch as they can't beat openers they might as well get out of the way. But this is entirely wrong, and contrary to the etiquette of poker. It is unfair to the other players. Bet, fold, check, or raise in turn—and insist that the others do likewise.

so you will inevitably lose. If, occasionally, you wish to indulge yourself it is permissible to draw to a smaller pair, but I still earnestly advise against staying on such holdings. In the first place, the odds are only 4 in 10 that you will improve your hand, and thus you are automatically lost 6 out of 10 times because you can't beat openers. On the other occasions, the opener or someone else may also improve (or had a strong enough hand to begin with) and you will lose to it. If you draw to fours and catch a pair of sevens, and the opener draws three cards and bets, you can hardly call and are almost certainly beaten.

Other times, another player will draw to a pair and catch a third making three of a kind. Suppose you hold sixes and catch a third six. The opener draws one card and bets. You are forced to call, on the chance that he holds only two pairs. Usually he will have three of a kind (when he bets)—and must have held them from the beginning and tried to hide his hand by drawing only one card and thus giving the impression he held two pairs. Or, he may have drawn to two pairs and filled. One other possibility is that, for example, he originally held J-8-7-4 of spades and jack of clubs and split his openers to draw for the flush. If he caught a spade, your three sixes will simply cost you an additional quarter or half dollar—or whatever he bets. The same things can happen if you stayed with aces and improved, but at least you weren't definitely beaten before the draw.

Unfortunately, however, the average player gets his kicks out of playing rather than folding, and so he stays and plays in far too many hands. Or, he may just remember the times when he caught—when, for example, he drew to a pair of deuces and caught two queens and another deuce. This draw he remembers. It's too bad he can't forget it, because in the course of his playing it will cost him many times as much as it won for him.

It's up to you

In the final analysis, it is the player himself who must handle the cards and throw in the money, and no matter how sane and sensible your arguments may be, they won't cut any ice with the man who is determined to play bad poker. Conquer your curiosity lest it cost you too much money! If you hang around and draw to low pairs when you should have folded, you may get a few kicks, but you'll walk away from the game poorer than you otherwise would. And I can only repeat the statement in the Introduction: this book is for the player who wants to win at poker—not the man who wants a good time. There's nothing I can tell the man who wants some kicks and nothing else out of poker, but if the man who is anxious to improve his play will abide by the principles stated herein, he will minimize his losses.

The exception mentioned above is the case in which it is permissible for a player to stay and draw to a small pair because there is enough money in the pot to justify the investment. Suppose you are playing a game in which the ante is a quarter, and you can open for a quarter and bet a half dollar after the draw. For three rounds no one holds openers, and the cards are dealt again, each time with another quarter ante. By the fourth round you have a dollar invested in the pot. Someone opens and several other players stay. When it comes around to you, stay holding any pair. It will cost only another twenty-five cents, and you stand to win in a proportion more favorable than the odds on your improving your hand. If you stayed with threes and caught a third one and two other players plus the openers stayed, with none of them holding more than two pairs after the draw, you will win, and at good odds.

On the other hand, if someone opens and everyone folds, it is downright foolish for you to stay and draw to anything less than kings yourself, because you don't stand to win much if you do win, and you will lose just as heavily as if there were half a dozen players. My own play is never to stay with less than a pair of aces in hands in which someone opens and the others fold. When it comes round to me, I fold kings or less, because the investment isn't worth while. Sitting on the opener's left I may stay with a pair of jacks or better, and if then the others fold I am stuck and can only hope to improve.

CHAPTER 5

Five-card stud

Five-card stud poker is the great gambling game—the favorite of the big professional card players who play for high stakes. Played in table stakes poker, it offers unparalleled bluffing opportunities and chances for the canny psychologist to make a killing at the expense of his less alert opponents.

When played in limit poker five-card stud takes on a different form entirely. Frequently, it is little more than showdown, and this is the reason that while it retains its popularity as the king of table stakes gambling games, it is often replaced by seven-card stud in limit poker.

In five-card stud, you are constantly playing to make an ace in the hole or a small pair stand up. It is very difficult to run a bluff, because you can count on someone to keep you honest. The cost of calling is so small that the other players will call automatically, unless they can see a better hand on the table. The differences in the two games—table stakes and limit poker—may be seen in the following example:

You have a king showing, with an ace in the hole. Another player, B, shows a king. C shows a seven. The other hands show small cards. B bets, say $4.00. The seven bumps, making it $20. You will probably fold, even though you may be holding the high hand. But, if the first king bets a quarter, and the seven makes it half a dollar, you stay, thinking that the man with the seven may be bumping on the strength of an ace in the hole, rather than a pair of sevens.

General rules

Certain rules may be laid down for general practice:

1. Don't stay unless you have a higher card in the hole than any card showing. This is not an infallible rule, of course, but it should be generally observed. Sometimes you will be higher than any save the bettor. In such instances stay.

2. Raise immediately with an ace in the hole or with any smaller pair wired. Your plan must be to build up the pot you expect to win, and, at the same time, to try to make whatever you are holding at that moment stand up. You do not want the other players staying in, drawing against you, unless you have aces or kings. Too often you will be outdrawn.

3. With a high pair—say, queens—bump at the first opportunity, but do not necessarily bump back if you, in turn, are raised, even though the raiser may have a weaker hand. Let us suppose you have queens wired. Player A on your right shows a king. B shows an eight. The other cards vary from six to jack. A bets a quarter. You make it a half. C, with a jack, calls. B makes it 75 cents. Two others fold. A, with his king, calls. Your proper play is to call.

The reason for such a play is this: if you bump again, you are definitely placed with queens and will be unable to get any more action out of the hand—unless someone catches a higher pair. The temptation to re-raise and to continue doing so as long as anyone will give you a play is strong, but it is not good poker. The situation you are now in is this: B probably has an eight in the hole. Conceivably he could have an ace, and raised, thinking you might have a king in the hole, for your raise. But this is quite unlikely. More probably he has the pair. When you don't re-raise, he figures you for an ace in the hole, and thinks his pair of eights is a high hand.

Building the pot

By only calling you will keep C in the pot, whereas a raise would be almost certain to drop him unless he had jacks wired. Thus he is kept in. If, on the next round, A is still high, he will check unless he has paired up. Your proper play is to bet. If B raises, call. The raise may drop A—or your bet may drop C—but it is necessary to build up a pot, and betting when you feel sure you will catch a raise is one of the best ways of sweetening the pot and, at the same time, directing attention away from yourself, because the others will be watching the raiser especially. If, on the next round, no one helps, and the king checks, check, too. This is a sandbagging check, for now that the limit is 50 cents, instead of a quarter, you are in a position to bleed the others with your queens. If you bet, B may only call. If he bets, raise. If C has improved and bets, and B either calls or raises, your proper play is to bump. If C bets, he will probably show several cards higher than eight, and B will be likely to call only, feeling his eights are no longer high. But, unless a pair shows in any of the hands, and its holder bets aggressively, you are safe in bumping—and should do so. This is particularly true if the pair that shows is higher than eights but lower than queens. Be wary of betting from a player who shows a pair lower than eights. In view of the betting thus far, whoever holds the low pair will know that B probably has eights, and if he bets into B or raises B it will surely mean he has a second pair, having paired his hole card.

On the last round of betting, after the final cards have been dealt, assuming no one helps, the players will probably check to you. You may as well bet in this situation—on the chance that you will have a caller. The pair of eights (B) is almost sure to call. The others will probably fold, unless they can beat eights. For, while B's pair of eights don't show, the betting has been such that there is little doubt as to his holding.

Play of two pairs

If you should happen to catch a small second pair on the last card, so that you now show a pair of fives, let us say, I suggest that you check the hand, hoping for a bet. If you bet, you probably won't get more than one call—unless someone has two pairs—as everyone will remember your strong raises the previous rounds, and they may figure you for two pairs. But if you check, they may think you were raising on an ace in the hole after all (remember: except for the possibility that B has eights there is no reason to believe ace high won't win this hand), and sometimes you will get a bet, either from

B or from one of the other players with a pair. This is not likely, but possible, and the only way you will be able to get the last drop of profit from the hand. If you bet your hand, it is unlikely that anybody will call, for they will place you with two pairs. If, on the other hand, you check and somebody bets, you can raise, and even if you aren't called you've managed to win the amount of the bet.

This is an example of the way to sweeten a pot you expect to win. Had you failed to bet it properly your winnings would have been a good deal less. You have been able to bump twice (and a third time if anyone bets into you after the last card), and once you have bet, knowing you would probably catch a raise from B. Had you kicked B back again on the very first round, every future round would have been checked to you (because everyone will be certain you have queens) and you would get no action. Then, when your second pair shows, the hand is absolutely washed up.

So make your bets with care, calculating their effect on others, and raise at the proper moment. Don't be too aggressive, as you will defeat your own ends. Anytime you can get someone else to do your betting, so much the better. It protects your hand. Remember that the moment you bet heavily and raise at every opportunity, you are advertising your hand, and you will rob it of the money winning strength it possesses provided it is properly handled.

Don't raise from spite

Don't let any personal considerations interfere with your betting. If you don't like one of the players, try to get his shirt, but don't let that dislike lead you to make bets and raises from spite. In the hand just described, if you don't like B, you will be especially tempted to raise him back in the first round—because you know you have him beat. But to re-raise is poor poker. The other players will invariably gang up on the aggressive raiser, not dishonestly, but by the simple expedient of checking to him every round. He will then bet and they will call. Unless someone catches a stronger hand, he receives no play. By moving more slowly and seeming to back down when a pair would raise you tend to disguise your holding, and B will proceed with the assumption that he holds the whip hand.

Or, put it this way: eliminate, for the moment, the other players.

By re-raising on the first round, you get an additional quarter from B—and that is all the extra money you will get the entire hand from him, for he will figure you for queens and call all of your bets but not raise. By forfeiting this quarter on the first round, you make it up on the second round of betting (by betting and letting him raise) and will get an additional fifty cents on the fourth round by sandbagging —with a possibility of something even more on the fifth round. In addition, your first round re-raise will either drive the other players out immediately or on the next round. The ability to extract the maximum possible amount from every winning hand is an earmark of the good poker player, and it explains why he can hold indifferent cards throughout the evening and go home a winner.

CHAPTER 6

Seven-card stud

Seven-card stud poker offers many opportunities to the good card reader that neither draw nor five-card stud afford. It is a game played a great deal in limit poker—often replacing five-card—because the latter game is more suited for table stakes poker. Too often five-card stud in limit poker tends to be a game of showdown, with few opportunities for the psychology and bluffing that it possesses in the big game.

Seven-card stud is a game in which there are three cards down and four up. Thus, a player may hold four of a kind or a full house without showing a pair; or a straight or flush with only two of its cards showing. It requires a lot of card reading ability if you are to play it and come out ahead. Inevitably, there will be hands in which you will be unable to guess what a man is holding from the cards in front of him and must draw your inferences from his betting. If he bets and raises heavily when showing nothing—and particularly when strong possibilities show on the table against him—you may expect him to be loaded, and should be most careful about calling or raising him back.

An illustrative hand

Let us assume you show a king, nine, and a pair of fours, and in the hole you have a king, queen, and jack. Kings up is a good hand and will win the average round of seven-card stud. If a player against you shows a deuce, five, nine, and queen, in different suits, your proper play is to bet your kings up (although if you have only the pair of fours, you should naturally check). If the player showing nothing raises, your proper play is to call, and under no circumstances to raise. With a king, queen, four in the hole, giving you fours full, you should, of course, bump back.

When you bet, your opponent, who, we will say, holds a pair of fives and a three in the hole, figures you for two pairs and is justified in bumping. Even if you hold a third four in the hole, his three fives will win. But, the moment you raise him back he figures you for a straight (with a Q-J-10 in the hole) or, possibly, a full house. This is the way his reasoning will go: to bet at all you must have two pairs, otherwise you would have checked. He raises. When you re-raise him, it indicates clearly to him that you can beat three of a kind, for the reason that you know he would not raise with two pairs (with queens up he would only have called, fearing kings up) and he must therefore have at least three of a kind. If both hands have three of a kind, the hand with the fours is almost certain to be low, consequently, the man holding it would never raise on the strength of it, only call. So, when you re-raise, he can only call, even with a queen-high straight. He knows you have at least a king-high straight, and, quite likely, a full house.

The second man, with the three fives, saves himself an additional round of betting by carefully reading the cards and drawing the right conclusion. In the course of an evening, card reading will play a decisive part in the play, preventing those who see they are probably beaten from making unnecessary raises and calls, and helping those who hold powerful hidden hands to sweeten the pot.

Watch all cards

It is particularly important in seven-card stud to watch all of the cards that fall and to remember the cards that are folded during the play. Let's take an obvious example: suppose A holds a pair of tens and a five, and B has a five, an ace, and a six. One hand, already folded, showed a ten and six up, and you hold an ace, queen, four, with an ace and a five in the hole. The fourth player, C, shows a nine, eight, six. The tens bet, and all of the players stay. On the next round, you catch a four, A catches a five, C, with his possible straight, catches a three, and B catches a ten. The two pair bet; the ace high hand folds. The possible straight—open on both ends—raises. Your proper play is to raise, too. If the two pair raises, regardless of what the possible straight does, you raise back with your aces up. And you continue to raise so long as either of the other players raises.

Why? Because all their cards are dead. This may seem rather simple when it is laid out in this manner, but the fact is it constitutes a most important part of your play and can hardly be overemphasized.

In the hand just discussed, C is almost certainly raising on the come. When he catches a seven on the sixth card, it leaves him open at both ends, and he pushes the hand, confident that his straight will roll in. The man with two pair likewise bets on the come, knowing that he can win the hand with a full house, if it comes in, regardless of whether the straight man catches. You raise at every opportunity because you know you hold the best hand at that time, and you must bleed it for all it's worth.

Had the first two players watched the cards they would have checked in turn and simply called your bet. The reason for this is that each of them would have known there was only one chance for him to catch. The man with the possible straight needs a ten or a five. He should have noticed that two tens already folded, and, with the pair of tens in the exposed hand, tens are dead. Only a five can help him. But, here again he can see a pair of fives in front of him, and one five has been folded. Only the case five will give him his straight. By the same reasoning, only the case five can fill the man with two pairs, because he should know that his tens are dead and that one five has been folded.

You know all this, too, and can carry it one step further, because you have the case five in the hole. Thus, you know that the one man cannot catch a straight, and the other man cannot fill up (unless he has a third pair in the hole and catches to it). Your hand of aces up is therefore the whip hand, going into the last card, and will, in all probability, win the pot. Further, you have a full house open, too, and all but one of your cards are live, to the best of your knowledge. No four has shown anywhere, and only one ace has appeared.

Other possibilities

There is one other possibility that ought to be considered, too. The man showing the possible straight may have three of a kind, e.g., a pair of sixes in the hole. Thinking over the betting you should recall when he raised. If he had a pair of sevens, eights, or nines in the hole, he would have raised earlier—as soon as his three of a kind came in. But he didn't raise, only called, even though he was in a good spot to raise had he so desired. He didn't raise until after the six fell on the sixth round. Thus you surmise he may have raised with three sixes or with a straight open on both ends. But, each of the folded hands held a six, and therefore you know the raiser can't hold three sixes and may therefore feel fairly confident that he is bumping on the come. The likelihood of his holding three of a kind is remote, in view of the way he bet. It is conceivable, of course, that he does have, say, three eights, and has been sitting back with them. But this is a matter which you, as a player with some familiarity with his style of game, must decide for yourself.

Regarding the player with the two pairs, even if he does hold a third pair in the hole he can't beat aces up yet, because the highest holding he could have at this stage is kings up (he can't have aces up, too, because a third ace was already shown). It is possible, of course, that you will be outdrawn. Perhaps the man with tens up has a pair of queens in the hole and will catch a queen on the seventh card to fill him. Or, the man with the possible straight may have a seven or eight in the hole and catch the seven or eight to make three of a kind and win. But these are risks you must be prepared to take. They are carefully calculated risks, for you have been able to eliminate many of the possibilities of their hands. And, in any event, you may catch the case ace on the seventh card—and that will take care of everything very nicely.

It seemed to me to be necessary to labor this point of card reading and remembering all cards, because it is often the ability to practice just such principles as these that sends you home a winner. After the seventh round, you win with aces up. Both of your opponents may grouse about their "bad" luck—though they should have known better—and they may say you were lucky when you go home a winner. But the fact is, you're a better poker player, and, in the long run, you will win a whole lot more in this game than you are going to lose.

The poker winner doesn't perform any miracles. His luck may be only average. But he will win because he makes the most of his cards, building up the pots he expects to win, and staying out of those he is almost certain to lose. In addition, he plays with caution, reading the cards carefully, and frequently calling where a rasher player would have raised. It is these factors that distinguish the fine player from the average, the consistent (though sometimes, of course, small) winner from the man who wins when the cards are running to him and loses when they are falling elsewhere.

CHAPTER 7

Strategy and tactics in stud

Let us suppose that you are playing five-card stud, and with a
ten in the hole, catch first a king, and after it a six, a jack, and
on the last card another six. Two other players have stayed. One shows
an ace, queen, nine, and six, and the other an ace, jack, ten, and five.
The proper play for you is to check your pair of sixes. They are
exposed. If you bet and neither of the other players can beat sixes,
you will have no callers. Thus you can't possibly gain on the hand by
betting. If, on the other hand, either of the other two players can
beat sixes, you will be called—or, perhaps, even bumped—and stand
to lose at least the amount of your bet. Simple though this rule seems,
it is violated constantly by poker players.

Re-arranging your hand slightly, let us suppose that you have one
of the sixes in the hole and the ten showing. If the man with the ace-
queen (who would be high if your pair didn't show) checks and so
does the man with the ace–jack, your proper play is to bet. But if
either of these players bets, you should only call, as a rule. You may
or may not bump, depending on factors which can't very well be discussed here (e.g., your knowledge of the style of play of your opponents). If the man with the ace–queen bets and the man with the ace–
jack bumps, your proper play is to call. The second man may have a
king in the hole and thus feel he has the high hand. But, under no
circumstances should you do anything more than call. If the second
bettor has a pair he will probably bump, and his pair is going to be

higher than yours in three out of four instances (aces, jacks, or tens) and it would be a mistake to bump him back.

Play of two pairs

Let us now suppose that with the king, jack, and pair of sixes up you have a jack in the hole. If no pair shows up in any of the other hands you have a certain winner, as the highest possible holding in any hand against you would be one pair. The proper procedure is now to bet. If anyone bumps, bump him back. You will be able to do this only once in the hand, of course, as your re-raise immediately places you with two pairs. But it is correct to bet your hand, unless you hope to sandbag. If you check and someone bets, you can raise—although it is problematical whether, having been raised, your opponent will even call your hand. He can see sixes. If sixes check and he bets his aces and gets bumped, he may possibly call, but he will certainly not raise.

In limit poker it is very difficult to carry off a bluff successfully, because the cost of keeping anyone honest is not too great. Your best opportunities for bluffing will come when you show (in seven-card stud) three cards in the same suit and raise—then catch a fourth. The other players will figure you for a probable flush, although you may not have another spade in the hole to match the three you have up. In the face of a probable flush and maximum betting—with one round sandbagged, perhaps—they will be inclined to drop unless their hands are definitely promising. But you will never be able to drive two pairs or three of a kind out of the game under any circumstances, for the reason that if they catch they are filled up and will beat your "flush." You may fold a possible straight in someone's hand by betting in this fashion, as your flush appears to be in and will beat their straight should it arrive.

You will also find bluffing opportunities in draw poker, when the opener takes three cards and checks. Often he holds only his openers, let us say queens, and a bet from you will make him think long and hard about calling—unless, of course, he is one of those players who calls every such bet on principle. You will find that you can peg the various players and their habits if you are alert, and this is of vital importance.

A bluffing play

Let us say, for example, that in a hand of seven-card stud, the player on your right shows three spades and the nine of hearts. The player on your left shows a pair of sixes, a ten, and a four; your hand shows a queen, jack, and a pair of fives, and in the hole, you have a ten and a deuce. The other players are folded. This hand may give you an opportunity to run one of the few bluffs that a limit poker game offers. Let us suppose that the man with the sixes checks, and the man with the three-flush bets. If you wish to run a bluff, raise. Unless the man with sixes has another pair, the bump may drop him, as he can see your pair and will probably figure you for another pair along with it, or, possibly, three of a kind. Thus he figures himself beaten as things stand and must improve on the last card to beat you. And he also knows that the bettor has a possible flush that will beat him whether he catches or not if it comes in. Rather than call the raise he may fold his sixes.

The strategy was this: you worked on the assumption that the possible flush has yet to come in, that the player was betting on the come. If he catches, you are beaten. On the other hand—and this is the crux of the matter—if he doesn't catch, his hand will be worthless. Thus, if he doesn't flush and you can drive the man with the high hand (the sixes) out of the game, you will win with your fives (again assuming that you don't improve on the last card). If you can't drive the sixes out or the possible flush catches, you are beaten, of course, but this is the risk that any bluff involves.

The important factor in this bluff is your location—between the man with the high hand and the man betting on the come. The strategy does not work out under other circumstances. If, for example, the sixes bet and the flusher calls or bumps, you would be better advised to drop out than try to run a bluff, because the man with sixes may well have another pair already—or even more. Under the circumstances just mentioned, your hand can safely call a modest bet, but should fold if the flusher bumps. You are at best next-to-high hand, and may easily wind up as low man. If the flushers bet and the sixes bump, you fold. The flusher may kick back (if his flush is already in, or he is the sort of player who has unlimited confidence in his ability to catch) and you will be caught in the middle with the weakest hand. If both players check, you check, too. You could never drive them out with a bet, and it is better to take the free card, hoping you improve and they don't.

Timing is important

It is well to remember that timing is a most important consideration in bluffing in limit poker. Where, in table stakes or pot limit poker, you can carry through a bluff on the strength of the size of your bet, in limit poker the cost of seeing you or staying in can never be made prohibitive, and consequently you cannot expect to drive anyone out by the sheer weight of your bet. Instead, you must choose the right moment for bluffing. Let us say that the game is five-card stud. Everyone antes and you catch a ten up and have an ace in the hole. The player on your right is high, with a queen up, and he bets the limit, say 25 cents. Making it 50 cents at once may well drive most or all of the others out of the game. The object of your raise was to drive the other players out of the hand. And such a raise should not be confused with the bump you make to build the pot. Let us suppose you have kings wired, and the man on your left is the first bettor, with an ace showing. He bets and everyone calls. You bump. This is a raise designed to build up a pot which you confidently expect to win. You raise as last man because all of those who have already tossed in a quarter are likely to throw in another one to protect the first, rather than fold their hands.

Rules

1. A bet to fold other hands should be made in the form of a bump before they have got much money tied up in the hand. Thus, it might be made immediately after a bet by a player on your right. In a dollar limit game, if the player on your right bets a quarter and you make it a dollar and a quarter, you are likely to fold those whose turn to bet hasn't come yet.

2. Bets to sweeten pots that you expect to win should be made at a time when other players are already involved in the pot and in the particular round of betting concerned so that they will feel compelled

to stay around and protect their investment. Sandbagging is never a means of driving others out of the pot. It is a means of getting them to contribute the maximum amount possible to the round of betting.

The third type of raising is tied up with the bluff, and has already been dealt with. There is no other type of raise that can be justified. The player who raises from spite or from habit or to liven things up, with none of the three specific purposes of the raise in mind, will find his losses increased and his winnings reduced, because promiscuous raising is invariably expensive.

CHAPTER 8

When to fold

The poker player who learns when to get out of a hand and gets out has come a long way toward mastery of this complex game. The same cannot be said for the man who knows when to get out, all right, but stays just the same. The reason a good player can hold rather bad cards and still go home a winner is that he knows how to build up the pots he wins and he stays out of those he has no right to be in.

Everybody knows the player who came to play, and you can't get him out with a howitzer. He's going to see seven cards, come what may. At some time or other, however, the rest of us have learned or will learn to overcome our desires to participate in every hand to the very end. You must develop a certain ruthlessness and cold-blooded approach to your cards. If they haven't strong possibilities, fold them up and wait till the next round. For the habitual stayer, this is hard advice to follow, but once he has begun to learn, the added incentive of increased winnings will keep him contented.

Folding in five-card stud

The question of when to fold is so broad that it would take hundreds of examples to answer it fully. Every hand poses its own special problems. But generally speaking, the following points are applicable:

1. In five-card stud, fold immediately unless your hole card is higher than any card you can see. If it is higher than any card except that of the first bettor, you might be justified in staying with it for one more round. The only other holding that you can safely stay on is a wired pair.

Remember that much of the strength of your hand in five-card stud comes from the hole card. If you can pair it, you stand a good chance of winning the pot. If you pair an up card, most of the others will get out, unless they hold pairs, too. But with your hole card paired you show nothing, and the others are encouraged to stay. This, of course, affords the best opportunities to build a pot.

Having stayed one round, fold as soon as higher cards than your hole card appear—unless you catch high up cards. In other words, fold as soon as you can see that you are beaten. Stud is not a game in which it pays to stay on the chance of outdrawing someone with a better hand. The idea is to get out of all pots that you aren't going to win—and to get out as soon as possible.

Try to make an ace in the hole stand up early in the hand. The longer others stay against your ace, the better are your chances of being outdrawn. Remember that the chances of there being a pair in the five cards are almost as good as the chances that there will be no pair. Thus, you must push that ace, and fold it up as soon as a pair appears. This is the reason you raise immediately with an ace in the hole if you can drive others out by doing so—that is, if you are on the original bettor's immediate left.

But the moment better cards than yours appear, fold. Save your money for the hands when you are high. At any time someone shows a better hand than you have, or his betting indicates that he has more than you do, drop out of the pot. Never stay to outdraw anybody. If you have a pair of sixes and have been betting them, and somebody catches eights, don't stay in to outdraw him unless you are already committed heavily in the pot and must thus protect your previous investment.

One final word about five-card stud. If you hold K-9-5 with an 8 in the hole, and the king makes you high, I suggest you check the round of betting to see what the others do. If you bet and somebody raises, you can't call. If nobody bets, you can feel some assurance that you are going into the last card with the high hand. But don't bet when you can't call a raise. With this holding, call any bet from a chronic bluffer. But it is better to sit tight with a weak hand (though it may be high at the time) and to see the next card as cheaply as possible, rather than to bet and be forced out if somebody bumps. By checking, you can call a bet—if one is made—and see the last card for a minimum cost. Thus, you achieve the same effect as you would by betting and having everybody call—as far as building a pot is concerned. If, on the other hand, the others check, too, you know you went in with the best hand. By playing it this way you are assured of seeing that last card without paying too much for it. This is another example of saving your money for the good hands to come. King-high may win this particular pot—but it would be reckless to bet the hand on this assumption. Much better to try to squeak by with the king-high—which will win fewer five-card stud hands than it will lose. Check it.

Folding in seven-card stud

2. In seven-card stud, there are only three holdings that will justify you seeing a fourth card, as a rule. You should have either a pair (or three of a kind), or three cards to a straight or flush. With any lesser holding you are well-advised to fold. Holding three high cards that offer a straight and flush possibilities—e.g., the king and eight of hearts and the queen of clubs—you might see a fourth card, provided there are no raises on the opening round. Such a holding offers chances of a high two-pair, and this will usually win in seven-card stud. But, if aces and kings show in other hands, or your cards are paired by up-cards in other hands, fold. And likewise fold with any lesser holding. You will save money.

Having a good enough hand to see a fourth card, fold after the next round is dealt, unless (1) you help your hand, or (2) you stayed originally with a pair. Holding a pair it is well to stick around until other, higher pairs show, or until the betting indicates that other higher pairs are in play. It is a mistake to stay in poker when you are at least reasonably sure somebody has you beaten. The only possible exception would be a hand which offered many chances such as 2-4-5-6-7-9 or 4-4-5-6-7-7, if four of the cards were of the same suit. These holdings are worth staying on even though three of a kind or a higher two pair may be out against you (provided sevens and fours, threes and eights, and the flush suit are still pretty much alive).

Unless you, too, are strong, drop out as soon as other players show signs of strength. I can only repeat that the idea in poker is to win the pots you stay on and get out of those you don't figure to win. Otherwise you fritter away the money you've won on your good hands by hanging around on the bad ones. And so you will win on nights when you are catching and lose on the nights when you are missing. The point of this book is to help you win all the time.

Folding in draw

3. Draw offers very few problems. If the pot is opened, don't stay with less than queens. If there are raises, don't draw to two pairs, unless you have jacks up or better. If a man on your right opens and you bump with two pairs, and the opener draws one card after calling or bumping you back, throw away the lower of your two pairs and draw to the higher pair and an ace kicker, if you have an ace, or to the pair alone. With kings up or aces up originally, you would take the one card under these circumstances. But with a lesser holding, you must make your try to improve. Watch to see if opener throws in his discard or puts it aside. He may be splitting openers to draw to a straight or flush because of your raise.

If you open with two small pair and somebody bumps, throw away the smaller pair and take three cards. It is no good drawing to your two pair against a high two pair or better. You can improve only to a full house, and the chances of filling are 4 in 47, or about 1 in 12. On the other hand, the chances of your catching three of a kind on a three-card draw are 1 in 8, which is better for you than trying to fill. In addition, three of a kind figures to win against the raiser— unless he fills.

Fold a four-flush or bobtail straight unless at least three others have stayed with the first, or four with the second holding. Sometimes, of course, you will be sitting next to the opener with a four-flush. If you can discern no signs of their intentions by watching those who have still to bet, don't hesitate to let the hand go. Fold it up and forget it. But, if this is a liberal game in which players often stay to draw to small pairs, you would be justified in calling the opener. Such a call will help the others stay, because it will make it more worth their while, and, in addition, you know in advance they will stay if they have anything to draw to.

Catching to flushes and straights

I don't recommend staying with a four-straight, open on both ends, unless at least two players have already stayed and there are yet two or three to be heard from. With the flush you may expect to catch once in every five draws you make for it, roughly, whereas you will make the straight once in every six times you try for it. From these figures you will readily see the importance of keeping out of pots in which only one or two players are staying. However, whether or not it is profitable to draw to such holdings will depend on factors that can't be discussed here, such as the size of the ante, and the size of the opening bet, etc. I will cite one example:

You are sitting with a four-flush. The ante was 25 cents, and the man on your left opens for half a dollar. This is a six-man game, and two others stay. This means that besides your own quarter ante there is $2.75 in the pot. If you call, you will have invested 75 cents—something more than a quarter of the pot. If you hit, the rate of your being paid off will be less than 4 to 1 (discounting bets after the draw which will be, at best, 3 to 1) and your chances of hitting are 9 in 47—or 5 to 1. Not exactly favorable odds, but worth a try. So, when it gets around to you, toss in your half a buck and have a go at it—unless you are losing and can't stand it. Then by all means fold and save money for a better hand.

With a small two pair, if there is a raise before the betting reaches you, fold. Chances are the raiser has at least a higher two pair, and you are almost sure to be beaten.

CHAPTER 9

Poker psychology

Psychology in poker will vary to such a degree that it is almost impossible to lay down binding rules. However, if you are alert you cannot help noticing certain habits and mannerisms of the other players. You will find, for example, that A invariably draws to any pair, regardless of how small it may be. B, on the other hand, will never draw to less than jacks. Thus, you know certain facts that should not be forgotten when playing with either of these men. Most players are a great deal more consistent in their play than they think they are. They do not—as this book urges you to do—sometimes hold a kicker and sometimes draw to the pair only. They may think that they ought to mix up their draws a little, so as to confuse the others, but the fact is that most players don't get beyond the stage of thinking about it. This is because they want to play every holding to win. So, they make whichever draw they prefer. If they think it is correct to hold a kicker, they do so. If they think it better to draw three cards to a pair, they do so. The thought might pass through their minds that it is a good policy to be inconsistent, but they decide to vary their game on some other hand and not on this one.

In five-card stud, some players will usually bump with an ace in the hole, but only call with a wired pair. They are anxious to drive everybody out in the first case, making their ace stand up, whereas with the pair they want the others to hang around because they feel their holding will win. It is most important to observe and learn such characteristics in play. Suppose you hold a king up and an ace in the hole. A, on your left, shows an ace and bets. B, sitting between A and yourself, shows an eight and raises. What you do with your ace–king will depend on what you know about B. If he is an average player, you fold. If he is an erratic or poor player, you call—and may even raise.

The reasons are these: if B is an average player, he would not raise on an ace in the hole because an ace shows against him, and if A has a nine or higher in the hole, B is raising a stronger hand than his own. This play is so obviously bad that the average player, B, would not raise. When he does bump under these circumstances it will almost invariably indicate a pair of eights. If he does have eights, you have no business hanging around, hence you fold.

The weak or erratic player

However, if B is an erratic or poor player, he may have an ace in the hole. Some players are so completely gamblers that they will raise with the ace–eight on the chance that A has no higher than an eight-spot in the hole. The chances are about even that A is eight or less, in which case B feels the issue will be determined by the cards to come, and he is willing to gamble his luck against A. This is the sort of play you can expect from the erratic, aggressive player, who likes to liven things up with frequent raises. If B is such a player, you, too, may raise, for you are holding the best hand—to your knowledge— at this point. Furthermore, your raise will lead the others to think you may have kings, and they will treat you with respect through the rest of the round, possibly checking to you every time.

If B is a fool, his raise may show a pair or it may show an ace in the hole. If the latter, he has simply ignored A's ace, feeling, perhaps, that any *ace* in the hole rates a raise. (Remember that the poor player knows less about building a pot than the good one. He will frequently advertise his hand by heavy betting, when a more astute player would mask the holding with calls instead of raises. The play of most dubs lacks subtlety. You can usually figure them for whatever holding is most obvious or most likely.) In this particular instance, a pair of eights is B's most probable holding (although if A does not show an ace, this changes matters considerably).

The amplifications of such a situation are endless. I mention it here simply to stress the importance of watching the others in the game and learning their style of play. It is a mistake to simply play the cards. Without exception all fine poker players possess the sensitivity and insight to detect and infer. It is their ability to estimate correctly the other players that enables them to build the pots they win. Simple mathematics and common sense keep a man from staying on hands when he should fold. And this is one of the two basic principles of winning poker. But the other one is harder to master. It takes an understanding of human nature generally and of your present opponents in particular to build the pots you are going to win.

Watch every player

When you have folded early and are watching the betting of those still playing, look at all of the hands after the call and not just the winner. When a man who raised early is beaten at the end, see what he raised on—provided of course the hand was bet and called or checked out so that you have the right to see his holding, regardless of whether it won. It will help you form a mental picture of his play. It is well to note what a man didn't raise on, always relating such a fact to the particular circumstances of the hand in question. Thus, a man who might ordinarily bet or raise, checks or calls with a potentially strong hand because he thinks somebody else will do his betting for him. Virtually every check, bet, or raise, by every player in every hand, is indicative of something. Nobody will be able to see and remember more than a small part of everything that goes on. But you should train yourself to stay constantly alert.

The fact that a man merely calls, when you know he would raise if he had anything, may mean he has nothing—or it may mean that the bettor was on his immediate right and he didn't want to risk driving the others out by raising at once. Thus, you must always modify your knowledge of a player's technique by the special circumstances of any given hand.

Here are some general considerations to keep in mind:

1. In draw, when a man raises and stands pat after three or four have stayed in front of him, it is more likely that he actually is pat (i.e., holds a straight or flush or is full) than it is that he has two pairs or, in extreme cases, nothing at all and is bluffing. The reason for this is that he knows that he cannot expect to bluff out all of the stayers ahead of him. With three or four others drawing against him, two pairs may not stand up. Hence, he would be more likely to take one card to his two pairs, if that were his holding, or not even try to bluff if he has nothing.

Is he pat—or bluffing?

On the other hand, if he sits on the opener's immediate left, calls and then stands pat, your estimate of his holding will depend on the number of players who stayed in back of him. Again, it is unlikely that he would try to run a bluff with the prospects of three or four callers. Usually, when he bluffs under these circumstances, he is holding a pair but decides not to draw to it when he notices that there are at most two other players. On the chance that neither of these held more than a pair, he stands pat and will bet the limit when the opener checks to him. His standing pat after failing to raise seems perfectly proper, because it would be a mistake to raise with a strong hand on the opener's immediate left. Such a raise would tend to drop the other players, and this is precisely what a man with a strong hand does not want. So the others will not feel his simple call was unusual.

I said that the man who makes this play usually holds a pair. The reason for this is that he does not decide to bluff until he sees that he is going to have two or less players. After all, it would be silly to call with *nothing,* preparatory to a bluff, when he has no idea what the four or five players still to be heard from are going to do (or when three or four have already stayed). In table stakes poker this is another matter altogether, and his bluff may be very successful. But in limit poker it is no good to plan a bluff such as this in advance. If the man has two pairs or better, he is not bluffing in the strictest sense (trying to win the pot with nothing), but is simply masking his hand by refusing to draw to it. Inasmuch as he may be going in with the strongest holding if he has two pairs or better, this cannot be considered a genuine bluff.

The other holding is one pair. It can be anything from aces to deuces. The man decides to stay and draw to his holding, so he calls when the pot is opened. Then, when he sees the others dropping out so that there are no more than two left, he decides to run a bluff and stands pat with his pair. Such a bluff is based on the hope that neither of the other players went in with more than a single pair and that neither will improve. Regardless of the skill with which the play is handled, you cannot expect to bluff out either of the men who improves his pair. Not at limit poker. They may be suspicious of your standing pat from the first, and the moment they help their pair they can be expected to call.

Watch exposed cards

2. When you evaluate another player's holding, always bear in mind what he may know of your hand. For example, if in seven-card stud you hold a flush, with three of the cards exposed, and another player showing nothing raises your bet, you had better call, not re-raise. No matter how unpromising his up-cards appear, he is almost surely full. Your flush is probably in. He can see this. His raise indicates that he can beat a flush.

That, of course, is an obvious example. There are many less simple instances that occur. You must always put yourself in the position of your opponents and determine the degree to which your hand is exposed. Bear in mind that they look your cards over before betting. If, in seven-card stud you show a pair of aces, and the other aces show elsewhere, you must be wary of the raise of a man who shows a small pair (or no pair), even though you have aces up. The reason for this is that even though your second pair does not show, they figure you have it when you bet. The man who raises is saying that he can beat aces up. Presumably he has three of a kind. He knows you don't hold a third ace. Figuring you for aces up, he raises. You can call but should never re-raise.

The way you bet will depend, therefore, not only on what you believe the other players are holding, but also on the appearance of your own cards. Let us say, in formulating a rule, that you hold a flush. The extent to which you are willing to push this flush will depend on whether you show two or three of the cards that make it up, and on whether or not your up-cards make it appear that you have any lesser holding. When you have a flush you will show either two, three, or four of its cards. If you have four you are not going to get any play—unless somebody is full. With three of the suit showing, you will know that the others are placing you with a probable flush. But, with only two cards showing—particularly if you also show a small pair—your hand is about as well disguised as a flush can be in seven-card stud. The small pair tends to direct the other players away from your flush possibility.

Don't bet on the come

3. Do not, as a rule, bet on the come. Some gamblers like the excitement of betting on a bobtail straight or a four-flush, and they argue that so doing is a legitimate way of building a pot. However, it too often results in killing off a potentially big money-making hand before it can be properly exploited. If, for example, your first three cards in seven-card stud are clubs, and you catch a club on the fourth card and raise, the other players will look at your two clubs that show and figure you are betting a four-flush on the come. Thereafter, they will only check to you if you catch a fifth club. A hand that offered many sandbagging and other raising chances was smothered before it had a chance.

On the other side of the picture, it must be said that it is difficult to bluff anybody out in seven-card stud on the chance that you hold a flush. Anybody, that is, who has anything. You can't bet enough. If you could bluff with some reasonable expectancy of carrying it through, it would be worthwhile to push the four-flush, because you would figure to have a good chance of winning even if it didn't arrive, and what you would win on the successful bluffs would more than compensate you for what you would lose (by betting a minimum amount each round) in those instances when you push it and it comes in. Unfortunately, however, you cannot expect to run the bluff at limit poker, and in the long run you will lose money.

4. Speaking of bluffing—as I have throughout this book—it is always well to remember that (1) you cannot expect to run a bluff for a large pot in limit poker, and (2) more successful bluffs are run in seven-card stud, when a player has something, but not as much as he appears to have, and in draw than are carried through in five-card stud. This last offers chances of running an immediate bluff to win the ante, but once play has progressed into later rounds, you can

always count on somebody calling unless he can see that he's beaten. And if he's beaten, it's not a bluff.

The bluffed man is always weak

In poker, it is never the potential strength of somebody else's cards that enables him to bluff you; it is the weakness of your own hand. A player who holds something is likely to call—if for no other reason, out of deference to his own cards, which he has seen win many a pot. Many successful bluffs are run against weak hands by still weaker ones. A man having opened with jacks and failed to improve is tempted to throw in the hand rather than call the bet of another player who took two or three cards. For some reason he seems to call the one-card draw hands when they bet more often than the others, perhaps because he feels it more likely that they are trying to bluff.

Many poker players are prone to congratulate themselves at having run a successful bluff, when, in fact, they actually had the strongest hand, no matter how weak it may have been. They weren't called because no one had anything to call with.

In twenty-odd years of poker playing, I have never seen anybody —master or fool—run a successful bluff against a holding of three of a kind or better in limit poker. In addition, it is difficult to force out any player with two pairs, as long as there are cards yet to come, because no matter how remote the chances may be, he still feels that he may fill up. It is usually easier to bluff the expert rather than the average player—but the expert will quickly learn the chronic bluffer's methods and will repeatedly capitalize this knowledge later in the evening.

CHAPTER 10

Illustrative hands

The following hands—one each of draw, five- and seven-
card stud—are included as examples. The analysis of the
motives for betting is, I think, fairly exhaustive. Much of the reasoning will be familiar to some readers. But I doubt if more than a few
will think of all the possibilities that are outlined. And the average
player will learn something if he studies the cards and the reasons for
betting. Every reason is deducible from the exposed cards and from
the betting. This is no double-dummy affair where one can hardly be
expected to find the right answers without knowing holdings which,
in actual play, would be unknown to him.

It is difficult, if not impossible, to lay down any laws, or make
dogmatic statements that this is the way it should be done. Holding
these cards and in these situations, various players would bet differ-
ently, perhaps. But, I have tried to show the proper play and to indicate where the man who would have done something else was making
his mistake.

In order to work the greatest number of situations and possibilities
into each of the three examples, strong hands have been set up. Of
course, one rarely finds such holdings bumping up against each other
in one deal in a six-handed game.

I suggest that you get a deck of cards and lay out these hands,
turning the up-cards in order and betting each round—then check

your answers with the book. I repeat, close study of the betting in these hands will repay almost all poker players. It will help them understand the art of building a pot, when to call, raise, and fold, and something of the art of card reading.

Draw

PLAYER	HAND DEALT					CARDS DRAWN		
A	8♡	7◇	6♣	5◇	3♠	4♣		
B	A♠	A♣	10◇	4♠	2◇	9♣	6♡	5♠
C	J◇	J♣	J♠	9♡	8◇	10♣	10♠	
D	Q♡	Q♣	7♠	7♣	5♡	A◇		
E	K♡	J♡	7♡	2♡	5♣	10♡		
F	K♠	Q♠	8♠	8♣	3◇	NONE		

CARDS TO RIGHT OF LIGHT VERTICAL LINE INDICATE DISCARDS

DEALER: A

GAME: Draw. 20-cent ante
Open for a dollar
Bet $1.50 after the draw

B opens
C calls
D raises
E calls
F folds
A calls
B calls
C raises
everyone calls

SEATING ARRANGEMENT

A
F
B
E
C
D

Notes

1. C will kill his hand if he raises immediately after the opener. He will drop players who might otherwise stay—not on this particular hand, perhaps, but as a rule. His hand is strong, and he figures to win the pot. Thus, he wants the others to stay. The best way to keep them in is to call. Sitting where F or A do, with the same hand, and with B opening, he raises.

2. D's raise is correct. He wants to drive the others out and knows he must do it before the draw, because there is little likelihood he will improve with the draw. The chances of his filling up are 4 in 47, or, roughly, 12 to 1. He bumps with two pairs at any time he feels the raise will fold others in the hand; he does not bump when most or all of the others are already in for the amount of the opener and, therefore, likely to see the raise, unless the amount of the opener's bet was small—say 25 cents, and he can make it $1.75. This great difference may tend to fold the others, as they will figure it is better to lose the quarter they have already bet outright than to gamble another $1.50. And this always excepts those with strong or potentially strong hands. The only original stayers you can expect to fold with a late raise are the men who have called with a pair. All others, including four-flushes and four-straights, are going to stay, because they figure to win if they improve.

3. E's stay is OK. Three others are already in, with two more yet to be heard from. He figures his flush will win if it comes in, and he calls. But he does not consider raising, as this would be an improper bet. If you insist on raising on a four-flush do so only when five others have already stayed. My advice is never to raise on a four-flush, unless there are six already in.

4. With four stayers ahead of him, A also calls. If he hits his bobtail straight he figures to win the hand. He should not, in my opinion, raise on a bobtail straight, even if five players have stayed ahead of him. Needless to say, he would be making a foolish mistake to stay if he had to catch on the inside for the straight. Both E and A fold if, for example, B opens, C calls, and D and F fold.

5. B, already involved, calls, though he could fold if he so wished.

6. Now is the perfect moment for the raise, and C makes it. Everybody is already committed to the point where another raise will keep them in. C feels he has the strongest hand—or, in any case, a powerful hand—and the raise is certainly justified.

7. D cannot raise again. He isn't going to drive many—if any—out, and there is reason to believe hands stronger than his are out. He knows there are sure to be one-card draws to straights and flushes and to two pairs, such as his own holding. The chances are decidedly against his improving. Under the circumstances he can only call.

8. Again B could fold if he wished.

After the draw the betting goes:
B checks; C checks; D checks; E bets; A calls; B folds; C raises; D folds; E calls; A folds.

1. C checks, hoping that one of the one-card draws came in or that somebody caught something. If he draws three cards and fills he can safely bet and count on a raise from anybody who connected on a one-card draw. However, after making a strategic raise in the opening round and then betting after drawing two cards, he will have few callers and no raisers. Better to check and hope somebody else will bet.

2. E figures C for three of a kind, hence the earlier raise. He figures D for two pairs, recalling that D was the original raiser. E feels it is unlikely that D caught, else he would bet. Too many have already checked for D to sandbag at this point. Thus, E bets his flush.

3. There is nothing A would rather do than raise, but, knowing E made a one-card draw and bet, he knows he is probably beaten by a higher straight or a flush (or possibly a full house). He can only call, and curse silently because he actually caught his straight on a hand it wouldn't win.

4. B folds. Some of these guys may be bluffing, but they all aren't.

5. A logical raise. If E drew to a higher two pair and filled up, C is due for a beating, but otherwise he is the winner. If A were full he would raise E, there being no point in worrying about the checkers any longer, as they will probably fold anyway in turn.

6. D folds even if C only calls. But with C out of the picture it is proper for D to call with his queens up, despite the two one-card draws. Both may have two pairs smaller than queens up.

7. In my opinion, E can now fold. But it is useless trying to convince any poker player that he should fold a flush in draw. E knows C took two cards. He is aware, therefore, that C does not hold a flush or straight. He knows, further, that C made a strategic raise on the first round. This, together with the two-card draw, indicates he went in with three of a kind. He now raises a bet by a one-card draw that was called by another one-card draw. There can be no doubt that C is full. So why, thinks E, should I contribute another $1.50 to verify my deduction? Unfortunately, the flush cannot be resisted, and E calls. When he does so, A folds. If E should fold, A figures that he was trying to bluff and will, therefore, keep C honest.

Thus, if you want to split hairs, C's last bet should go uncalled. With a flush and a straight out, however, this is more than unlikely. It is unheard-of.

Note that *restraint* was the keynote of C's play in building a fat pot. Twice he held off when he could have raised, calling the first time and checking the second. Both times his play paid dividends. This is not to say that every time you restrain an impulse to raise you are doing the right thing or that even if it is the proper play you will get the kind of action you want. But the fact remains that your abiding by the correct standards will, in the long run, pay you off better than any violations of the basic principles.

A word about bluffing: bluff (in limit poker) only enough to assure yourself of callers on those hands when you really want callers. The hand illustrated above is an example. Nobody will call C after the last raise if C has the reputation of a man who never bluffs. Do not bluff more than the minimum number of times necessary to create this impression. Bluffing more than this minimum will cost you more than you'll make the times you are called. Bluffing less than this minimum will make it unlikely that you'll have any callers when you want them.

The idea is to be caught bluffing occasionally—otherwise, you will not have the callers when you want them. Your bluff must be exposed. Then the others will never know when you're bluffing and when you aren't, and they will call your bets when you want them to. If you run a few successful bluffs, keep trying until you are caught a few times. Remember that if you run a successful bluff, no one knew you were bluffing, otherwise somebody would have called. And inasmuch as it is important to have the reputation of a player who will try to run an occasional bluff, it is necessary that you be caught a few times. But don't strain for it, in any case! Nothing is gained by being too obvious.

Five-card stud

PLAYER	HOLE CARD	EXPOSED CARDS			
		2	3	4	5
A	K♢	4♡	6♢	A♠	NONE
B	J♠	9♣	J♡	5♡	8♢
C	A♡	3♣	A♢*	7♠*	4♣*
D	7♣	K♡*	Q♢	7♢	10♠
E	5♣	7♡	NONE	NONE	NONE
F	2♢	5♠	NONE	NONE	NONE

*Bets first on that round.

SEATING ARRANGEMENT

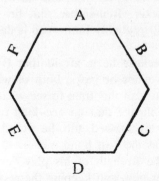

GAME: Five-card stud. Quarter–half, with a half dollar bet permitted on an open pair or before and after the last card.

The betting

ROUND ONE: D bets; E and F fold; A, B, and C call.

ROUND TWO: C bets; D and A call; B raises; C calls; D and A call.

Notes: It would be a mistake for C to raise in his position. A pair of aces is a strong hand, and it ought to win this pot. If C re-raises,

D and A will probably be forced out of the hand. C wants to save his raising until such time as each raise will cost the others twice as much—and until he is in a better position to raise, i.e., after the others are all in and pretty well committed to stick it out to protect their investment. A could drop if he wished.

ROUND THREE: C bets; D and A call; B raises; C and D call; A folds.

Notes: 1. C bets into the raiser, hoping for another raise. He can sweeten the pot this way with a little more subtlety than by sand-bagging, as this latter course places him with aces at once and means he cannot again hope for a chance to raise. This is an important consideration, with another 50-cent round coming up. The strategy of betting into a raiser, when you know you have him beat but show nothing, is often very effective. It appears to the others to be careless of you, for they (thinking you have nothing) will expect you to have remembered that the man you're betting into raised on the previous round. By betting—not aggressively or forcefully—you will get the raiser to do the pot building for you, and he will leap at the chance, figuring he has a sucker. Remember that he thinks he holds the strongest hand. He will probably bump and is delighted at the chance to do so.

2. D only calls, because he is afraid that B has a pair. If B is paired it will be with nines or jacks, both of which are higher than sevens. He is willing to call this time to see what B will do.

3. A calls, on the chance that an ace–king may still be high and win the hand. If his king showed, too, he would fold.

4. B, figuring he has the best hand, raises.

5. C only calls. The strength of his play lies in letting the other hand do his betting for him, and keeping the rest of the players in.

6. D calls, with misgivings. He figures B has him beat. The only other possibility he can see—aside from a bluff—is that B has an ace in the hole and hopes ace–jack will stand up. The fact that A stayed with a 4 and a 6 indicates a high hole card or a low pair.

7. A folds. He places B with a pair and does not intend to stay in an effort to outdraw him, particularly when two of his four cards are too low to win, even if they were paired, and there are both another ace and another king showing. Some may argue that he should stay, having stuck around this long, but I think he is better off getting out.

No point in throwing good money after bad. That half dollar he saves will come in handy another time when he has good cause to stay in a hand.

ROUND FOUR: C bets; D folds; B calls.

Notes: **1.** No point now in C sandbagging. If he checks, D will probably check, and when B bets and he raises, it is almost certain D will fold, and even possible that B won't call. Some will argue that by checking and then raising C will do better, but I don't think so. Here he assures himself of a sure 50 cents—and perhaps a dollar, if D should call. If B should raise again, he can re-raise, thus making a possibility of $1.50 to $2.00. But if he checks and raises, D is certain to fold, and B will either call or fold, making $1.00 the maximum that he can make. Also, if he checks it is not at all unlikely that the round will be checked.

2. D places C with aces as soon as he bets. Otherwise, he feels, C would check, because the best he could have would be either threes or fours. D knows C can't have a pair of sevens, as he holds two himself and recalls that E folded a seven on the first round. The bet seems to place C definitely with aces. Also, he fears B, in view of the last raise.

3. Conceivably, B could bump once, but he remembers that C has already bet into him once—after he had raised the previous round—and he thinks C may be looking for another raise. Also, he does not bump because the whole play by C may be a bluff, and if it is a bluff, C will re-raise, forcing him to call. But, if B raises, C will re-raise if he holds aces, and thus the betting will follow the same pattern as it would if C were bluffing—except that C would win this time instead of B. The chances of C bluffing are slim as they are in all limit poker, and B figures that C actually has the aces. He knows that A folded an ace the previous round. But that leaves two aces still unaccounted for.

In addition, B knows that his own hand is, in a sense, exposed. In view of his earlier raises, he has announced that he has either nines, jacks, or an ace in the hole. (If he had fives or eights, that would mean he has a five or an eight in the hole, and neither makes his hand strong enough to justify his raise in the second round.)

B also knows that everything he knows is also known to C. The only way C can beat B's probable nines or jacks is with an ace in the hole. The chances that C is bluffing are slight. For if C were bluffing, he would have taken advantage of B's earlier raises to re-raise, thus driving the others out. C bet into B on the third round—after an earlier raise by B—but only called when B raised. Not a bluffing bet. B figures C was using him to sweeten the pot, betting into him when he was certain he held the stronger hand and believed B would bump.

This bet of C's is not a bluffing bet, for a bluffer in C's shoes would know he would be called by B, who had raised twice previously. Thus, B could fold, and properly, if he wished to do so—virtually certain that C had aces. But it takes a hardened gambler to fold jacks in the face of nothing, particularly when the cost of calling is only fifty cents and he already has a goodly amount invested in the pot. And so B tosses in his half dollar with one hand and folds his cards with the other.

Seven-card stud (See chart on opposite page)

ROUND ONE: E bets; F folds; A calls; B calls; C and D call.

Notes: A should not raise on his pair of eights. It is likely to drop other players, and he is not interested in driving anybody out at this time. The fact that F has folded in front of him makes it even more important, psychologically, for A to refrain from raising. A bump might fold everyone still to be heard from, whereupon A stands to win only E's original bet—provided E doesn't stay and beat him!

B calls for the same reasons outlined above. A raise at this juncture is not profitable. Better to hold the others in by calling and see what happens.

D's call is minimal, and no one would blame him for folding. With three cards to a straight, however, he cannot be censured too severely for staying. With a 6-5-4 holding he definitely should see at least one more card.

ROUND TWO: C, D, and E check; A bets; B calls; C, D, and E call.

Notes: C cannot bet his possible flush, even with only one other heart showing. Betting on the come is sometimes admissible, but certainly not in this instance. It is a risky business to ever bet a three-card flush, and I do not recommend it.

(Continue reading at bottom of page 83)

PLAYER	HOLE	CARDS	THESE CARDS ARE EXPOSED				7 (down)
			3	4	5	6	
A	8◇	Q♠	8♡	6◇	10◇	Q♡	J♣
B	7◇	7♡	9♣	4♣	4♠*	2♣*	7♣*
C	9♡	5♡	2♡	K◇*	6♡	9♠	A♡
D	8♠	4◇	5♣	6♣	A◇	7♠	J♡
E	A♠	K♡	Q♣*	9◇	K♠	4♡	NONE
F	3♠	5◇	10♣	NONE	NONE	NONE	NONE

*Has first bet in that round.

SEATING ARRANGEMENT

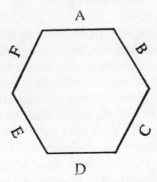

GAME: Seven-card stud; quarter–half, with half a dollar bet permitted on an open pair and on the last two rounds of betting (i.e., before and after the last card is dealt).

Despite catching another card to his straight, D ought not to bet, because he still needs to hit in the belly. And, while no sevens show, he should check, riding along as cheaply as possible until he comes in. With a bobtail straight, D could properly bet.

Again B should only call. He may figure A for a pair or for a straight working. If it is the latter, however, B is reassured by the pair of sevens he has in the hole. To raise on his sevens might fold the three who have previously checked, and the size of the pot does not warrant his trying to drive them out as yet. C calls—though folding if B had raised—and if his next card is not a heart or a king he must fold.

E has excellent chances for a high pair. He should not fold yet, although he, too, would have had to drop out if there had been a raise.

ROUND THREE: B bets; C and D call; E raises; A, B, C, and D all call.

Notes: C has a good call now, having caught a heart. Despite the fact that no seven has showed yet, D has a minimal call. He could safely drop out, if he wished. On the other hand, reassured by the absence of sevens and by the potential strength of the ace he just caught—no aces show, either—he calls.

E has a legitimate raise, for with one high pair already in, he thinks he may catch another and kings up will win the hand. In addition, there have been no previous raises, so he feels safe in raising. A's possible straight bothers him, particularly in view of A's free bet on the previous round. Nevertheless, he may as well bump now and give A a chance to re-raise, because if A is unable to bump he (E) probably holds the best hand and should build a pot. This raise is less a calculated risk than a gamble, but it is reasonable enough.

B must not raise. It will place him with two pairs or three of a kind, and he will drop at least two men, unless they are stronger than they look. The chances of his improving two pairs are slim, and in view of E's raise (which could show a straight, of course) it seems quite possible that there may be a stronger hand than his already in play. Even with three fours B should only call. It would not profit him to drop the two men on his left.

Again D could fold, if he wished, but he has been trapped by having the raise on his left. Already in for half the amount, and knowing there can be no further raises, D stays. If B had raised, too, D should fold.

ROUND FOUR: B and C check; D bets; E calls; A raises; B and C call; D raises; E folds; A, B, and C call.

Notes: B should not bet. His hand isn't strong, and one of his sevens and one of his fours have showed on this round. For C, to bet his four-flush on the come, even though strengthened by the pair of nines, would be unwise. While he can count only three hearts outside his own holding, he figures that nines up will not win this hand, and it would be foolish to push the flush. By checking, he knows the others will not notice his hand as closely as they would if he bet, and then if the flush does come in—a true hidden flush—he will be in a position to raise.

A feels pretty good about queens up, especially after E only calls D's bet. One queen shows in another hand, but no eight. Queens up will be a winner, he feels, unless E catches a second pair on the last card. (E's previous raise probably showed kings, although it may have showed a straight. A has one ten himself and knows F folded a ten—killing half of E's chances of having a ten in the hole for the straight.)

D must re-raise, although A could conceivably have a higher straight. The second raise folds E. To stay with kings only would be a costly mistake.

A now places D with a straight, or three sevens. The first is less likely, A feels, because three fours show, and he can account for two eights and three nines. Nevertheless, A is not too concerned about D's exact holding, for the reason that if he (A) fills up, he will beat what seems to be D's maximum holding of sevens full—and to hold this D has yet to catch—with his eights or queens full. And if A doesn't catch he figures he is beaten regardless of D's exact holding.

ROUND FIVE: B and C check; D bets; A calls; B raises; C raises; D calls; A folds; B raises; C calls; D folds.

Notes: B and C both sandbag, confident that the others will start the betting and they can raise. They are justified in doing this by the raises that have been made on previous rounds. Sandbagging is correct in both cases.

D bets, figuring to get a call from A and win easily.

A calls, thinking somebody had better keep D honest. He has no idea of the power on his left and expects both B and C to fold. If either looks as if he will call D, A drops out.

Both raises are correct. B's raise looks to C more like a flush than a full house, and holding an ace–high flush himself he feels he has a winner. He is also confident his hand will win because it is hidden. It is especially good that his ace is not exposed.

D has probably already counted the pot, and he must feel true despair as he calls. Nobody would blame him for folding, though one rarely sees a straight folded in poker. Clearly, B and C have hit on the last card, thinks D, and one of them—probably both—have him beaten.

B realizes that C can have a full house. Because his own hand looks like a flush, he knows C has at least a high flush—otherwise C would only have called. Still, B knows C can't have nines full, because he holds one nine and E folded one. (Nor, it might be added, although not important, could C have sixes full.) Also, remembering that E folded a king, B knows C can't have four of a kind, for between his own hand and D's, B can see a mate for each of C's up-cards. E's four of hearts eliminated any chance of a straight flush. Thus, of C's possible holdings, only kings full can beat B.

This reasoning leads B to conclude that C holds a flush, ace or king high, and his (B's) re-raise is not based on any idea that a full house is a strong hand that "ought" to win, but, rather, on sound deductions from careful card reading.

C now suspects the worst. He knows B can't have fours full, because two other fours have already appeared in other hands. Thus, he figures B for either a club flush or three of a kind in the hole, filling him up. If it is the flush, it is an almost certain winner if it is ace high—the reason being that of the unaccounted-for clubs, only the three-spot in B's hand would make it a lower flush than C's. With the ace and any club except the three, B's flush will be the winner.

C asks himself the important question: when B re-raises me, what does he think I have? And following the same line of thought outlined above, C decides that B has him figured for either a straight, a flush, or kings full. To raise again, he must be able to beat either of the first two.

So C concludes that B has three of a kind in the hole, filling him up; otherwise his re-raise would be unsound. C eliminates a possible bluff on the grounds that B would know either C or D would surely call. C calls.

D folds. To call with the straight would be foolish.

CHAPTER 11

Poker quiz

1. The game is draw. You are sitting second hand and are
dealt four spades. The man on your right opens. Do you call,
raise, or fold?

Answer: You can either fold or call, but should not raise under
any circumstances. Unless you think it likely (knowing the tendencies
of the other players towards liberality or tight play) that those following will call—at least three of them—you could, of course, fold.
If, on the other hand, you think three others or more will call, too,
you may probably call. Otherwise you are giving yourself the short
end of the odds.

2. Sitting sixth hand in the same game, and with the same holding,
the man on the dealer's left opens. The two following players fold,
and the fourth man calls. What should you do?

Answer: Fold. I know this is difficult advice to follow, but the fact
is that the odds on your catching do not warrant your drawing to the
flush against two or, at most, three other players. You will catch
your flush once in every five draws, roughly, and this does not warrant
drawing to it at less than 4 to 1 odds in the pot—and this means
four other stayers. At the same time, I know drawing to a four-flush
is one of the most attractive draws in poker, and I don't blame
those who can't resist it.

(The above advice applies also to a bobtail straight. Your chances of hitting such a straight are, roughly, 1 in 6, which means it is not quite so good a draw as a four-flush.)

3. You are the dealer in a hand of draw. You hold 9-8-6-5-2 in several suits. The man on your left opens, and three players stay. What should you do?

Answer: Fold. Your chances of hitting an inside straight are 4 in 47, or roughly 1 in 12. As a matter of cold fact, you should never draw to an inside straight. It is difficult to imagine normal circumstances in which such a draw is permissible, though one such possibility is cited below.

4. The game is draw poker. You are the dealer and hold A-K-K-Q-10. A player on your left opens. Two others call. You call. The first two players, one of them the opener, stand pat. The third man draws three cards. What is your correct draw?

Answer: Split the kings and draw for the inside straight. If the opener took cards and the second or third player stood pat, you should draw to the pair, on the chance that the pat hand is a bluff. On the other hand, the second man may actually have his pat hand, in which case he might have been afraid to raise lest he drive out the other players. However, in the instance mentioned above, if the second player were bluffing, he would have re-arranged his plans when the opener stood pat, because he would realize that he couldn't bluff the opener in a limit game. So, when he finds the opener standing pat, he would have drawn to the best holding he had. And the fact that he does stand pat indicates a pat hand—at least a straight—in this instance. Therefore, you should split the kings. But, to repeat, if the opener draws cards and the second man stands pat, you should draw to the kings. If the second or third man raises before the draw, your proper play is to fold.

5. Draw poker. You are sitting third hand and are dealt three aces. The man on your right opens. Do you call or raise?

Answer: Call. A raise will profit you very little as compared to the advantages of calling. Stifle your desire to push those aces. Showing restraint now will pay off later. A raise may fold every player who has still to bet. If even one of them calls—after you call—you figure to be as well off as you would be in raising. If several call, you should draw two cards, giving the impression that you are holding a kicker (for the others will figure that you couldn't have three of a kind, else you would have raised). If the opener bets and there are three stayers on your left, call only. A raise may drop them, and if even one calls you will probably be as well off as you would be by raising and dropping them, even with an additional call from the opener.

If only two or less have stayed on your left, raise the opener.

As a general rule, draw two cards to three of a kind. An exception might be in the case of your having opened the hand, where you might wish to give the impression of holding two pairs only. If you insist on drawing only one card to a high three of a kind, check, for this is the only way you can expect to milk the hand. If there is a bet from any hand that drew at least two cards, raise.

The disadvantage of drawing only one card to three of a kind when someone else has opened is that the opener and the others are likely to check to you, and you will have no opportunity to raise. If they bet into you, you can only call, for however reckless many poker players are, they usually respect a one-card draw and will bet into it only when they hold a flush or better.

6. Five-card stud. You are the dealer, and the man on your left gets an ace up on the first card. You catch an ace, too, and find one in the hole. The man on your left bets. Several others stay. What do you do?

Answer: Raise. The others will figure you for a king or queen in the hole, rather than aces wired. But, if the ace is on your right and bets, call only, so as to keep the others in. With a pair of aces you are not interested in driving the others out. Aces will win most hands of five-card stud. The more callers, the better for you. If, later, a pair shows somewhere and you can raise without folding too many others, by all means do so.

7. Five-card stud. You hold aces wired. A shows Q-J-10-8. B shows K-9-4-4. You show A-8-6-5. You have been betting, as high man, and the others have been calling. On the last card, B pairs and bets. You raise. A re-raises and B folds. What do you do?

Answer: Raise—but you may fold if A raises once again. The reasoning is this: A holds a higher pair. He can beat B's pair of fours, and he can beat any pair you may have, except aces. (B should have checked his fours of course. because he has nothing else. Should he check and you bet and A raises, you will be in the same situation and may properly re-raise.)

Chances are A has a pair of eights. If he held a pair of queens, jacks, or tens, he would be raised in an earlier round. He raises you, figuring that he can beat your small pair. Your re-raise shows aces very definitely. Therefore, if A raises you once more, you can figure him for the nine in the hole giving him his straight, and could, if you wished, fold the hand without another thought. Bear in mind that this applies only to limit poker, where, for example, each raise is for a quarter.

This hand illustrates one of my pet theories—which is that there are too many hands called in poker. In limit games, by careful card reading and by staying alert to the way the betting has progressed throughout the hand, you will be able to guess what your opponent is holding in either of the stud games. This is not an infallible rule, of course, because the seven-card game gives him three down cards. Card reading will not avail much in the case of, let us say, three of a kind in the hole, but you can deduce some such holding from the way the betting goes.

The illustrated hand should not be called, actually. Either A should drop when he is re-raised, or you should drop when A keeps bumping you. One time in a million, perhaps, A will raise, thinking you may have a king in the hole and are figuring an ace–king will win the pot. But A's proper play is only to call if he thinks this is the case. And no intelligent player in A's position would think your bet showed nothing more than an ace–king, because he would figure you would check with an ace–king rather than bet.

You know A figures you for a small pair maximum when he raises. Your re-raise shows aces, unmistakably. If he holds a straight, he will, of course, raise yet again—and go on all night if you will. His re-raise into aces could only mean that he holds a nine in the hole, inasmuch as most players would not attempt to run a bluff such as this for a quarter. They would know they could not carry it off.

Much will depend on the type of player A is. If he rarely or never bluffs, you ought to fold without hesitation. The fact that you have raised does not obligate you to call in the event you are raised back. If, on the other hand, A is capable of trying to bluff one out, it behooves you to call his re-raise.

Mix up your game. You can't afford to get the reputation of a man who doesn't call, because you will be bluffed right and left. But never hesitate to fold in the face of a holding which is almost certain to have you beat. Any player who brags that he has never been bluffed or chides you for possibly (or surely) allowing yourself to be bluffed is a poor poker player, and you'll have his shirt in time. And if that's not more important to you than having the reputation of a man who can't be bluffed, then you oughtn't to be playing poker— or not for more than pennies.

The above analysis is important. Study it over and absorb it. It will save a great deal of money for you. The man who understands when to fold and when to call has cleared one of the biggest obstacles in the path of poker excellence.

8. Draw poker. You hold a four straight flush and draw one card, catching a six-high straight flush. Another player draws two cards and bets. When you raise, he raises. Do you finally call?

Answer: No. With a two-card draw he can't have more than four of a kind. This simple example is given to support my argument that you must play the cards, not the player's attitude. No matter how confidently or aggressively he bets his hand—four aces, let us say— you know he can't beat you because he drew two cards. A man does not draw two cards except to a pair and kicker or three of a kind. His best possible holding still won't beat you.

9. Draw poker. The pot is opened and one man on the opener's immediate left has stayed when the betting reaches you. You hold three fives. You raise, and the other stayers call, each drawing one card. You draw two cards, catching two queens for a full house. The opener bets, and the second stayer folds. Do you call or raise?

Answer: Call. A raise would be injudicious with less than queens full. You are practically certain the opener has filled up, otherwise he would check. Your raise and two-card draw clearly places you with three of a kind. When the opener takes a card and bets into three of a kind, you can bet he is full. And in the case in point, he is virtually certain to have a higher full house than you have. There is always the temptation to raise on a full house, but you must have a great degree of flexibility to your play so that you don't make unsound raises. On this particular hand your full house is worth about as much as an eight-spot high: it is worthless.

Had the opener checked, after drawing one card, and the other stayer checked, too, you should bet, of course, but only call any raise. If the opener checked, and the other stayer bet, you might try one raise, on the assumption that he drew to a four-flush or a four-straight. First, though, decide whether he usually stays on the opener's immediate left with a four-flush or four-straight. If not, call only, as he probably filled two pairs. Do not, under any circumstances, raise if the opener appears to be ready to call. You'll win as much by calling (if the opener calls), and you run no risk of a re-raise. You will probably be safe in raising, because inasmuch as the bettor did not bump on the opening round—as he would likely have done if he held two pairs originally—the chances are that he drew to either a flush or straight.

When your betting has indicated your probable strength, and when your draw confirms this, you must be wary of bets into you and only call where you would otherwise raise. Few poker players are deliberately suicidal. They don't, as a rule, bet into one-card draws, unless they can stand a raise. When they present you with a perfect spot to raise them they usually want that raise so they can re-raise and you will do better to call.

Sequence of hands

It seems superfluous in a book of this kind to list the values of the various poker hands, but in case there should be any doubt, here they are:

ROYAL STRAIGHT FLUSH
STRAIGHT FLUSH
FOUR OF A KIND
FULL HOUSE
FLUSH
STRAIGHT
THREE OF A KIND
TWO PAIRS
ONE PAIR